ESCAPE TO REALITY - **GREATEST HITS, VOL. 4**

PAUL ELLIS

D1569366

KINGSPRESS
Birkenhead, New Zealand

Grace Remix: Escape to Reality Greatest Hits, Volume 4

ISBN: 978–1–927230–30–5
Copyright © 2015 by Paul Ellis

Published by KingsPress, Birkenhead, New Zealand. This title is also available as an ebook. Visit www.KingsPress.org for information.

Cover layout and design by Brad Wallace of bradwallaceimaging.com.

Version: 1.0 (August 2015)

Dedication: This is for all who ever heard grace mixed with law (especially those who heard it from me!) and now have to unlearn some stuff.

From E2R Readers

Paul Ellis is today's voice crying in the wilderness, proclaiming the beauty and freedom of grace in a world bound up with law. His insights have led me to a deeper understanding of what Jesus did for me 2000 years ago. His writing has demolished confusing teachings that plagued me for decades.
- Mike L., MSgt, USAF (ret.), Orlando, FL

I used to suffer badly from depression and anxiety. I was an atheist and I couldn't imagine God being able to help me. I was recommended Escape to Reality and it was Paul's article on the good news that truly saved me.
- Nath C., Stoke-on-Trent, United Kingdom

My wife and I grew up in the traditional Christian church with its teachings of saved by grace, live by law. We have found Escape to Reality to be a real blessing. Finally, we're hearing the gospel of grace without the religious teaching of rules and commands.
- Michael D., writer, Columbus OH

When I first began to understand the grace of the gospel of Jesus, I found that there were some scriptures that seemed contradictory. Paul Ellis tackles these difficult verses head-on and explains them through the lens of grace. I am extremely grateful to Paul for helping me to get a revelation of grace that makes more sense than any law-based message ever did.
- Bryan B., software engineer, Fort Worth, TX

For almost five years I have being reading Paul's articles. His teachings are kind, strong, and easily consumed. Through Escape to Reality, Jesus has set me free from many fearful beliefs that I had held since childhood — doctrine and Christian ideology that had me tied up in knots. After I stumbled across E2R, the lies began to unravel and I was exposed to the fantastic, enormous grace of Jesus. I am eternally grateful for Paul's role in helping me discover the truth.

- Connie-Louise A., public relations, Toowoomba, Australia

E2R has been such an encouragement to me. It has helped me change my entire perception of how to successfully walk this new creation life and, in turn, relate that to my congregation. Lives are being changed! Thanks Paul for all that you do!

- Andrew B., pastor, Fenton, MI

Paul Ellis and his books and blog are great blessings, especially with my questions about God, grace, and Christianity. I'm not just learning, but also unlearning. I will be forever grateful to God for your life, Paul, and I'm looking forward to years more of reading your writings.

- Love M., QA specialist, Philippines

Thank you, Paul for changing my thinking. After 40 years of wrong preaching and problems, I am now preaching the truth found in the grace message. Your weekly email teaching surely changed my ministry.

- Con B., pastor, Durban, South Africa

Contents

A word before   1

1.   What is the "whole" gospel?   7

2.   Your glorious new past   13

3.   Beware the dogs of law   19

4.   Is God sovereign?   27

5.   What about Hebrews 10:26?   35

6.   Don't listen to Job's friends   42

7.   Does God scourge us?   48

8.   Fear and trembling   55

9.   Three reasons why I don't preach "turn from sin"   62

10.   What is Biblical correction?   67

11.   Chop off your hand?! Was Jesus serious?   73

12.   Fear God who can throw you into hell?   82

13.   What is the fear of the Lord?   88

14.   James: Preacher of grace?   93

Bonus track...

15.   The X-Men gospel   97

A Word Before

This week our baby girl received her Australian citizenship certificate in the mail. She just became a little Aussie. This despite the fact that she has never been to Australia, she can't name the six states or the prime minister, and she doesn't know what a lamington is. She's never read "The Man from Snowy River," never enjoyed a Vegemite sandwich, and never seen an AFL Grand Final.

She has done none of the things that Australians do, yet she is, by law, 100 percent Australian with all the rights and privileges that entails.

The day you were placed into Christ, you became a brand-new citizen of the kingdom of God, with all the rights and privileges that entails. But like my daughter, you may not be enjoying all the benefits of your citizenship. In Christ you have received forgiveness, righteousness, and holiness, but you may not know that you are forgiven, righteous, and holy.

This is why the scriptures exhort us to be renewed in the spirit of our minds (Ephesians 4:23). That's another way of saying, "Change your thinking. Discover who you truly are. See yourself as heaven sees you, as a beloved child of God."

My daughter is already an Australian, but if she wants to live as an Australian, she will have to learn how to be one. Similarly, we need to learn how to walk and talk like citizens of a heavenly country. The Bible calls this working out our salvation and acknowledging every good thing that we have in Christ. We do none of these things to become citizens, but because we are citizens.

One day I may take my daughter to Australia and help her explore that amazing country, but that is nothing compared to the adventure of discovering who we are in Christ.

I met Jesus when I was a child, but it wasn't until I became an adult that I fully began to appreciate all that he has done for me. Several years ago I had what can only be described as a grace awakening. For the first time I understood what made the new covenant *new*, and I began to see myself as my heavenly Father sees me — as pleasing, acceptable, and dearly-loved. After that, everything changed.

Previously, I had been confused by a lot of stuff in the Bible. I had read it cover to cover, but much of it made little sense to me. The problem was I saw the Bible as an instruction manual when I should have been reading it to learn about Jesus (see Luke 24:27).

But after my grace awakening, everything came into sharp focus. I began to see Jesus on every page and in every chapter. Old, boring scriptures became new and full of life. The words hadn't changed but their meaning had. Obscure stories that I had dismissed as ancient history, sprang to life. Archaic laws, ancient proverbs, even the long lists of who begat who, came alive with fresh significance. "This is talking about Jesus!" I realized. "Every word of it points to him!"

Since I am one of those people who doesn't know what he is thinking until he sees it written down, I began to write what the Holy Spirit was showing me. I started sharing my thoughts online in a blog called Escape to Reality (E2R for short).

After five years, and half a million words covering more than 700 scriptures, and with 15,000 comments from readers, E2R had grown into one of the largest grace resource sites on the web. But it had also become an unnavigable mess. So I decided to go through the archives, pull out the best articles, and release them in a series of Greatest Hits. Volume 1 is called *Grace Disco*, Volume 2 is called *Grace Classics*, and Volume 3 is called *Grace Party*. You may be wondering why I named this volume, *Grace Remix*.

A remix is something old seen through new eyes. Here's an example. Before my grace awakening I interpreted much of Jesus' teachings as hyperbole. "Jesus is exaggerating to make a point. He's not seriously suggesting that we chop off our hands." That's the thin edge of a bad wedge. Dismiss some of Christ's teachings as hyperbole and we might as well dismiss them all. Grace has taught me to value everything that Jesus said, including his audacious message about chopping of hands. More on that in chapter 11.

Before I got grace I interpreted much of the Bible as dire warnings for misbehavior. "If I don't heed this scripture, I may be punished." That's the thin edge of another bad wedge. It'll lead you to trust in your own moral performance and fall from grace. More on that in chapters 3 and 7.

Before grace changed me, I was intimidated by many of the hard scriptures in the Bible. I didn't know what to do with them so I filed them in the too-hard basket. But grace has caused me to view that basket as a treasure chest. Tough scriptures like Matthew 10:28 ("Fear the One who can destroy both soul and body in hell") and Hebrews 10:26 ("If we deliberately keep on sinning after we have received the knowledge of the truth, expect raging fire!") no longer frighten me, they thrill me. More on those scriptures in chapters 5 and 12.

Before I got grace, Bible study was a drudge. Now it is a delight.

Before I got grace, I used to dread preaching because I never knew what to say. Now I have much to say. In the old days I used to leave my sermon preparation until late Saturday night. Now I leap out of bed each morning keen to write about all that God is showing me.

God has given me a new song and it is a remix. It's the timeless truths of scripture as seen through the lens of the new covenant. It's the ancient and eternal gospel of grace as seen through the eyes of the new man.

I'm no historian, but I understand that the remix movement was driven in part by DJs who put dance beats on top of old tunes to get people onto the dance floor. You would be sitting in a club and you would recognize a tune, but it sounded different. It was both familiar and fresh, and it made you want to dance.

Grace preachers are like those early DJs taking the old tunes of scripture and mixing them with the rhythms of the new creation.

This is what Jesus did. He took old scriptures about loving thy neighbor and mixed it into a new story about a priest, a Levite, and a Samaritan. It was old, it was new, and it was good. It filled people with joy. It changed the way they thought about God and his kingdom.

And that's why we're here – to renew our minds and discover all God has in store for us.

Some of the material on E2R has gone on to shape chapters in my various gospel books. However, most of the articles in this collection of greatest hits have not been published anywhere else.

As before, I have taken this opportunity to give them a bit of a polish, and after each you will find reflections and stories about how they came to be and how they were received.

How does this collection of greatest hits fit with the previous volumes? Like this:

Grace Disco – good news to make you dance
Grace Classics – good news that has stood the test of time
Grace Party – good news to make you celebrate
Grace Remix – good news to renew your mind

The articles in this collection of greatest hits are designed to put a new song in your heart and a jig in your step. The scriptures in here are old, but the song is new. It is the song of a heavenly country, whose citizen you are.

1. What is the "Whole" Gospel?

Heaven forbid that we preach half a gospel, but what is the *whole* gospel? Your answer to that question reveals your views on the finished work of the cross. For instance, whenever I proclaim the good news of God's unconditional love, I can just about guarantee that some serious person will pull me up for not preaching the *whole* gospel.

What they say: "We've got to preach the *whole counsel* of God, brother."

What they mean: "You should tell people they need to do stuff—repent, confess, turn from sin, work, etc.—to earn the free gifts of grace."

Earn the free gifts of grace?! What an absurd thing to say. It's like saying, "Children, pull out your piggy banks because Mommy and Daddy expect you to reimburse us for your Christmas presents." How ridiculous! How can you compensate God for his priceless gifts?

What is the "whole counsel" of God?

Paul told the Ephesians "I have not hesitated to proclaim to you the whole counsel of God" (Acts 20:27). Some translations say, the whole will of God. The whole counsel and the whole gospel are the same thing because God's will is always good news. He is not willing that any perish. He doesn't want anyone to be lost but desires all of us to come to him to receive new life.

So what is the whole counsel of God that Paul proclaimed? He tells us three verses earlier:

> However, I consider my life worth nothing to me; my only aim is to finish the race and complete the task the Lord Jesus has given me — *the task of testifying to the good news of God's grace*. (Acts 20:24, emphasis added)

The whole counsel of God is the gospel of his grace. Period.

"Just grace?!" says the serious man. Yes, grace and nothing but. Not grace-plus-your-confession, nor grace-plus-your-repentance — just grace.

"I can't accept that," says the serious man. Well, you wouldn't be the first person to have a problem with grace:

> The Pharisees and lawyers rejected the counsel of God… (Luke 7:30a, KJV)

Isn't that interesting — those who loved the law rejected God's counsel. Who else did the Pharisees and law-teachers reject? Jesus! Indeed, Jesus is the whole counsel of God. If you would preach the counsel, the whole counsel, and nothing but the counsel of God, then preach Jesus and nothing else. He is both the will of God made flesh and the means by which God's will comes to pass. Jesus is the Good News!

How not to preach the gospel

I will give you some practical handles on how to proclaim the whole gospel some other time, but let me finish here by showing you how *not* to preach the gospel: Add stuff to it.

If you take all the blessings of God — his love, favor, forgiveness, acceptance, healing, provision, deliverance, etc. — and tell people they must do stuff to merit them, then you are diluting the gospel of grace. You're preaching a mixed gospel where grace is no longer the whole gospel, but only a *part* of it.

Whenever we add things to the gospel of grace we dilute its strength and empty the cross of its power.

What do these gospel additives look like? I am sure you know them. They are called prayer and fasting, Bible study, the spiritual disciplines, tithes and offerings, Christian duty, the virtues, works of service, ministry, self-sacrifice, helps, missions, outreach, submission, sowing, etc. In the hands of graceless religion these good things become death-dealing burdens. If you think you must do them before God will bless you, you have fallen from grace as hard as any Galatian.

Religion is cruel

Imagine a thirsty man crawls out of the desert and you say to him, "Drink this, it is pure spring water."

That's good news for the thirsty man. He doesn't need to do anything except receive what you are offering. But if you ask that man to do something before you give him the drink, then it's no longer good news. It's torture.

Telling a thirsty man he must pray for an hour before he can drink is not good news. Nor is telling him that he must keep the rules and do what he's told. This isn't good news either. It's bad news. It's the religion of this world that derailed the Galatians, the Ephesians, the Laodiceans and many other churches since.

And telling him that the drink is free now but he must pay later is no different. In fact it's worse because you have given him a taste of real freedom before binding him with cords of obligation.

The good news is that grace is always free and if we drink it daily it will change us from the inside-out.

You want to see change in your life and the lives of others? Then follow Paul's lead and preach the whole undiluted gospel of grace without adding anything to it.

This emphasis on *what we must do before God will bless us* is poison in the water. The true gospel is additive-free. It's grace from start to finish.

Look to the cross—God has blessed us already! Look to the empty tomb—the work of saving and sanctifying you is finished. Believe it! Reach out and receive by faith the gift God has already given.

If you would preach the whole gospel then preach Christ alone. He is all you need.

A word after

A recent survey revealed that 71 percent of Americans agree with the statement that "an individual must contribute his or her own effort for personal salvation."[1] Most Christians would react to this by saying, "No, salvation has nothing to do with our effort, for we are saved by grace alone," and they would be right. Salvation is a gift from God, a blessing that is received by faith from start to finish.

Yet many of those same Christians say things like, "God won't forgive you unless you repent and confess. We're sanctified by keeping the law."

So even as they are trusting God to freely provide them with one blessing (salvation), they are relying on their own efforts for all the others. "You have to confess to be forgiven. You have to obey to be sanctified. You have to fast, pray, and do a bunch of other things before God will bless you."

The Bible declares that every blessing comes to us through Christ alone (Ephesians 1:3), yet many in the church don't believe it. They think "grace will get me in the door, but it's up to me to finish what Christ began." This is the Kool-Aid of DIY religion.

---

[1] Source: Ligonier Ministries (2014), "The State of Theology: Theological Awareness Benchmark Study," October 28, p.4, website: bit.ly/19DAx97, (accessed March 20, 2015).

I hear from people on an almost daily basis who are struggling to accept that God's grace is sufficient for *all* our needs. They see Jesus as their Redeemer and Savior but not their Righteousness and Holiness from God (1 Corinthians 1:30). They don't understand that Jesus is the complete package, the whole kit and caboodle. They've bought into a partial gospel—a gospel of salvation alone—but they haven't heard the whole gospel.

As we saw, a partial gospel puts some of the emphasis on you and what you must do before God will bless you, but the whole gospel puts the whole emphasis on Christ alone. It's a huge difference.

A partial gospel will turn you into a neurotic wreck, but the whole gospel will fill you with uncontainable joy. A partial gospel will burden you with impossible demands, but the whole gospel will set you free from unholy expectations. A partial gospel will leave you full of yourself, but the whole gospel, as one wise reader said to me, "is so full of Jesus that there's no room for anything else."

2. Your Glorious New Past

When you got saved you were probably told a lot of wonderful things about your future. "God has a wonderful plan for your life." You may have also been told some wonderful things about your present. "We're living in the kingdom now!" But you probably didn't hear too many wonderful things about your past. "It doesn't matter where you've come from or what you've come out of." If anything, you probably heard unpleasant things and warnings about your history. "Don't go back to Egypt!"

But God is not only the Lord of your present and future, he is also the Lord of your past. When you were born again, he gave you a brand new life complete with a brand new past. In him, you have a completely new history! And it begins at Calvary:

> I have been crucified with Christ and I no longer live, but Christ lives in me. (Galatians 2:20a)

When you were placed into Christ, you were placed into his death on the cross. In short, you died. This is one of the most important things that ever happened to you, yet many Christians are ignorant of it.

Just once I would like to hear a believer testify about their past like this: "I was born, I did some stuff, and then I died. I was crucified with Christ and the person I used to be no longer lives." That's basically what Paul is saying in Galatians 2.

We died with Christ so that we might live with him.

If you want to live the life that is Christ's, you need to answer three questions:

1. What did I lose at the cross?

At the cross your old self was crucified with Christ (Romans 6:6). The person you used to be apart from God — your "old man" — is dead so there's no point trying to reform him. If your old man gave you a bitter and painful past, then go dance on his grave because he's gone and he's not coming back.

What else did you lose?

Your sin has gone (Psalm 103:12), so has any relationship you might have had with the law (Romans 7:6). This means you can say goodbye to guilt and condemnation for there is no condemnation to those who are in Christ Jesus (Romans 8:1).

Rejection is also gone and if you can wrap your mind around the awesome love revealed to you through the cross, then you will find all fear of punishment has gone as well (1 John 4:18).

The world as you knew it is no more (Galatians 6:14). Your old sources of identity and security have been replaced with something infinitely better.

Any anxiety you may have about the future will go when you realize that you are in him and he has already overcome the world (John 16:33).

2. What did I gain after the cross?

At the cross you received peace with God and complete forgiveness (Colossians 2:13). When you were placed in Jesus, you gained his acceptance (Ephesians 1:6, KJV), his righteousness (Romans 1:17), his holiness (1 Corinthians 1:30), indeed, his eternal perfection (Hebrews 10:14).

That's wonderful! But wait, there's more.

As a result of the cross he gave you his life. Now Christ is your life (Colossians 3:4). You stand on his faith (Galatians 2:20), are filled with his Spirit (Romans 8:11), and you think the thoughts of his mind (1 Corinthians 2:16).

When you were born again you were made into a brand new creature (2 Corinthians 5:17). As he is so are you in this world (1 John 4:17), so obviously you do not have a sinful nature. You are not one person on Sunday and another on Monday. Sure, you can still walk after the flesh and reap corruption, but you are not defined by what you do. And when you do sin, you have an Advocate who speaks to the Father on your behalf (1 John 2:1).

But here's the thing; you no longer want to sin.

Because of the cross you have new desires and new aspirations. You used to be driven by the flesh but now you are led by the Spirit (Galatians 5:18). You are both more rested and more fruitful than you have ever been before.

Best of all, you've come home to your Father (1 John 3:1) and now enjoy the full rights of sonship (Galatians 3:26). Before the cross you may have feared God from a distance, but now you can approach his throne of grace with confidence (Hebrews 4:16).

Before the cross you were a beggar living off scraps from the king's table. But because of the cross your every need—whether for healing, deliverance, or provision—has been abundantly supplied according to his glorious riches in Christ Jesus (Philippians 4:19). You are now an ambassador and a royal priest of the most high king (1 Peter 2:9). And as his representative you have authority over sickness and demons. You shall lay hands on the sick and they will recover.

3. What did I retain after the cross?

As we have seen, you lost a lot and gained a lot at the cross. But on the day that you were born again, there were two things that you retained unchanged. First, your physical body did not change. You may have been healed, but your body is still subject to the effects of the fall. Although *you* were saved, your earthsuit is still getting older one year at a time, which is why we eagerly await "the redemption of our bodies" (Romans 8:23).

Second, beyond repenting and deciding to trust Jesus with your life, your way of thinking probably did not change. If you liked chocolate and Zumba classes before you were saved, then you probably liked chocolate and Zumba classes after you were saved.

The beginning of your new story

The instant you were born again, God changed just about everything there is to change about you. But one thing God left unchanged was your mind or your way of thinking. This is why some believers are struggling. Although they have been made new, they are still thinking old. They are acting like the person they used to be instead of the person they have become. They know how to walk in the way of the world, but they have not yet learned how to walk in the way of the Spirit.

In Christ, you are a brand new creation, but if you don't know it, you won't experience it. If you think you're still an old sinner, you'll act like an old sinner. As a man thinks, so he is.

Our thought patterns are shaped by our past. So which past are you identifying with? Your old man history or your new man history? In your thinking have you put off the old and put on the new?

Everything we need pertaining to life and godliness comes through our knowledge of him who called us (2 Peter 1:3). If you want to see breakthrough in your life, look to Jesus, look to the cross, and change the way you think. Tell yourself: "On the cross I died and the life which I now live in the flesh I live by the faith of the Son of God who loved me and gave himself for me."

This is the glorious beginning of your new story!

A word after

Growing up in the church I heard many testimonies of how sinful people had been before they met Christ. It almost became a competitive thing, to see who could have the most scandalous past. "You sold drugs? Big deal, I sold nuclear weapons to the North Koreans!"

You'd hear these exciting sin stories and they would all finish the same way. "Then I met Christ and I don't do that stuff anymore. I'm just a boring believer." Contrast that with the apostle Paul who considered his past achievements as dung and who barely mentioned his former life as a hunter of Christians. The best parts of Paul's story all came *after* he got saved.

If Christians lead dull lives, it's because they don't appreciate what happened to them at the cross. They think that Jesus merely made them *good*. They don't know that he made them *great*.

I wonder what would happen if we spent less time talking about the misdeeds of our past and more time talking about the great treasure God has placed within us.

Instead of reminiscing about the old man, we should just bury the fool and get busy living.

3. Beware the Dogs of Law

Have you ever noticed how Paul often warns us about those who preach another gospel? In just about every one of his letters there's a warning: "Watch out for those who put obstacles in your way contrary to what you have been taught" (Romans 16:17). "See to it that no one takes you captive through philosophy which depends on human tradition rather than Christ" (Colossians 2:8). "If anyone preaches a different gospel, let him be accursed" (Galatians 1:8). "Charge certain people not to teach false doctrines" (1 Timothy 1:3).

When warning about false preachers, and particularly those who seek to bring the saints back under law, Paul doesn't mince his words. "Watch out for those dogs" (Philippians 3:2). His animosity towards religious dogs may have been prompted by the disaster that fell upon the Galatians:

> I suspect you would never intend this, but this is what happens. When you attempt to live by your own religious plans and projects, you are cut off from Christ, you fall out of grace. (Galatians 5:4 MSG)

The Galatians never intended to cut themselves off from Christ, but this is what happens when you become seduced by dead works. One moment you're under grace, the next you're under law. One moment you're free, the next you're enslaved.

Maybe you're thinking, "It'll never happen to me." Yet many Christians are in danger of falling from grace into dead works. They are trying to get God to bless them in response to their performance.

If it happened to the Galatians it can happen to us. Below is a list of seven signposts or dogs that reveal whether you are walking in faith. To the extent that these dogs are barking, you are not in faith. You are in danger of falling from grace and back under law.

1. You always try to do the right thing

A preoccupation with doing the right thing is a classic sign that one has been eating from the Tree of the Knowledge of Good and Evil. To live by a code of conduct is inferior to the life Christ wants to live through us.

In choosing the wrong tree, Adam chose independence from God. An independent spirit wants to decide for himself and thus prefers rules to relationship. But someone under grace says, "I trust him from start to finish. He will lead me in the right path."

It's a cliché but your choice really is rules or relationship. You cannot reduce relationship to a set of rules. Live by the rules and you're setting yourself up for failure, for the law inflames sin which leads to death (Romans 7:5). Even when you do the right thing it'll be the wrong thing because you'll operating in an independent spirit instead of walking by faith.

But if you choose to abide in Christ, you'll find yourself doing the right thing at the right time every time.

2. You think we must do everything Jesus said

Jesus said "be perfect" (Matthew 5:48). How's that working out for you? If you can't score a perfect 10, then you've failed the test and there's no hope for God requires perfection and nothing less. But the good news is we have a perfect High Priest whose perfect sacrifice has given us perfect standing before God forever (Hebrews 10:14).

The new covenant of God's grace did not begin at Matthew 1:1, but at the cross when Christ's blood was shed for the forgiveness of sins (Matthew 26:28). Everything Jesus said was good, but not everything he said was for you. (For instance, much of Matthew 23 was directed at those "sons of hell" the Pharisees. You are not a son of hell.) If you fail to filter Jesus' words before the cross through his actions on the cross then you may have settled for an inferior covenant.

3. You think poverty is a good thing (it teaches character)

If poverty is a good thing, then abject poverty must be great. But there is nothing admirable about a twelve-year-old girl having to sell herself for food money or babies dying from preventable diseases. The devil wants you to think that poverty is a gift from God or that it is a controversial subject but it is not. Poverty is part of the curse, while prosperity is part of God's provision made available to us through the cross. (What do you think "blessing" means?)

A poverty mentality is a natural consequence of living under law, for the law constantly reminds us of our indebtedness. But grace reveals a God of the "more than enough."

Live under the "weak and beggarly elements" of the law (Galatians 4:9, KJV), and you'll end up weak and beggarly yourself. There's no such thing as a prosperity gospel, but neither is there a poverty gospel. There's only the gospel of Jesus Christ who became poor so that through him you might become rich (2 Corinthians 8:9). There was no lack in the garden and there's no poverty in heaven. If poverty is not God's will there, it is not his will here.

4. You think nothing will get done unless we first bind the strong man

A law mindset will have you thinking in terms of things *you must do*, even if they are things *Jesus has already done*. At the cross Jesus disarmed and triumphed over his enemies. Now it's our privilege to plunder the strong man's house and set the prisoners free.

To live under law is to say that Jesus can't do it, won't do it, or hasn't done it. But grace rejoices that the work Jesus came to do—which included taking down the devil—was completed at the cross. We empower a disarmed enemy when we believe him to be dangerous and in need of binding.

Instead of focusing on the enemy, look to Jesus who is your victory. Satan is already under his feet. Put him under yours.

5. You don't see yourself as righteous

Then you need to repent and believe the good news! Before the cross righteousness was demanded of sinful man (Deuteronomy 6:25). But at the cross righteousness was freely given (Romans 5:17).

The gospel of grace reveals the gift of righteousness that comes from God (Romans 1:17). God doesn't make you righteous because you are good, but because he is good!

If you don't see yourself as righteous, train your mind to agree with God's word: "God made him who had no sin to be sin for us, so that in him we might become the righteousness of God" (2 Corinthians 5:21). That's not describing a future event. That's describing what happened when you were placed into Christ.

Under first Adam you were literally a sinner; in last Adam, you are literally righteous. "If anyone is in Christ, he is a new creation; the old has gone, the new has come!" (2 Corinthians 5:17).

6. You don't see yourself as holy

Then you're in trouble because "without holiness no one will see the Lord" (Hebrews 12:14). Dead religion defines holiness in terms of behavior, but this definition falls short of the perfect holiness required by God. Just as you cannot make yourself righteous, neither can you make yourself holy. But thank God for Jesus who is "our righteousness, holiness and redemption" (1 Corinthians 1:30). It is by his sacrifice — not yours — that you have been sanctified (Hebrews 10:10).

Few would say the Corinthians acted holy, yet despite their bad behavior, Paul said they were "sanctified in Christ" (1 Corinthians 1:2).

Jesus is holy and righteous and in him *you* are holy and righteous. A law-preacher says you must strive to become holy. That's like saying, "I don't identify with Christ who is my holiness." But under grace we are exhorted to *be* holy (1 Peter 1:15), because that is what we are. We don't do to become, we do because we are.

7. You think you have disappointed God

Under law it's natural to think that you have disappointed God. No one, except Jesus, has ever lived up to the righteous requirements of the law. All fall short of God's glorious standard (Romans 3:23). But the happy truth is that it is impossible to disappoint

God. Disappointment results from unmet expectations and God doesn't have any. The word disappoint is not in his vocabulary and it barely appears in the Bible.

Before you were born your heavenly Father knew everything that you would ever say and do. He knew how long it would take you to come to the cross. He knew how many times you would stumble. He knew in advance when you would run like a coward and act like a dullard. He even knows about all the mistakes you haven't made yet. And knowing this he still loves you! Isn't he wonderful?

Under law it's natural to think of our shortcomings and project them as disappointments onto our heavenly Father. But grace opens our eyes to a good God who loves us with an unfailing love and who, knowing all our faults, chooses to remember them no more (Hebrews 8:12). The next time you do something dumb, don't listen to the lie that says you've disappointed him. Instead, rest in his shadowless love and rejoice!

A word after

A reader called Michael queried the second sign ("You think we must do everything Jesus said"). "Aren't we supposed to obey the commands of Jesus?" asked Michael. "Isn't that a sign that we love him?" Indeed it is. Obedience is a fruit of trust. It's the offspring of a loving relationship. It is because we know and enjoy the love of Christ that we can love others, preach the good news, heal the sick, cast out demons, and so forth.

Yet a law-minded person rarely does any of these things—when did you last hear good news from a legalist?—because they are operating from fear instead of love. They interpret Jesus' words as *commands that must be obeyed!* They fear the consequences of disobedience. They worry they will lose their reward or their salvation if they don't do what they are told. And since they aren't operating in faith they miss grace and curse all that they do. The only "reward" for performance-oriented religion is anxiety and stress.

When the Galatians fell from grace, Paul asked, "Where is the sense of blessing that you had?" (Galatians 4:15). A grace-filled life is a blessed life. A law-based life is a cursed one (Galatians 3:10). Which do you prefer?

Jesus spoke words that the whole world needs to hear, but what you hear in his words will reflect your heart. If you are confident of your own righteousness, you will hear condemning law. If you are in need of grace, you will hear grace.

Read Jesus' words as *commands that must be obeyed*, and you are setting yourself up for failure. You cannot succeed. But come to Jesus poor in spirit, hungry and thirsty for his righteousness, and you will be blessed (Matthew 5:3,6).

4. Is God Sovereign?

A friend of mine lost several million dollars in a bad investment. He is well into his seventies and this was his retirement money, so this is a big blow. How did he lose it? He took some bad financial advice from a dodgy analyst and put his money where he shouldn't have.

But my friend doesn't see it like that. He told me, "God is in control. I guess he didn't want me to have all that money." In other words, God is to blame for his loss.

When I heard this I was too stunned to speak, but my friend was just getting warmed up. "I'm like Job who suffered at God's hand. At least I can say, 'God gives and God takes away, blessed be the name of the Lord.'"

Well, isn't that just swell?

As I have explained elsewhere, Job was wrong about God being a thief and a killer.[2] Judging by the reaction *that* article stirred you'd think I was a heretic, but I was merely repeating something that Jesus and Paul said (see John 10:10 and Romans 11:29).

Today I want to go a little further and address three lies or half-truths that may need to be rooted out of your belief-set.

---

[2] See chapter 6, "Does God give and take away?" of *Grace Classics: Escape to Reality — Greatest Hits, Vol. 2.*

Lie #1: "God is in control of everything"

There is perhaps no more damaging lie than the belief that God is in control of everything and that he is the reason everything happens. You hear stuff like this all time.

"I got cancer but God is sovereign. He permitted this to happen to teach me something."

"God took my baby. I guess he needed another angel in heaven."

"I lost my job. God took it because I was enjoying it too much."

Statements like these are ignorant. How many people did Jesus give cancer to? How many people did he rob or kill? Jesus did none of these things yet some think his Father does them on a regular basis.

Jesus went around healing the sick, raising the dead, and preaching good news to the poor. If God were making people poor, sick, or dead, then the Father and the Son are a house divided. But he isn't and they're not.

If God was in control of everything, then he would be responsible for all the evil in our world – all the wars, killings, disease and destruction. But God is not the author of evil. In him there is no shadow at all.

The Bible never says God is in control. Instead, it says "the whole world is under the control of the evil one" (1 John 5:19). Much of the world is under the influence of evil. It remains captive to what the New Testament writers called the power of darkness.

Although Satan was defeated and disarmed at the cross, his influence persists wherever the light of the gospel does not shine.

The problem with thinking God is in control is that it makes us passive spectators in the ride of life. We'll just sit and take whatever life hands us saying, "*C'est la vie*. God is in control. Life will take care of it." Can you imagine how short the New Testament would be if Jesus and the apostles believed that?

The truth is that God is not in control of everything. The good news is that his sphere of influence increases as we, his children, shine in a dark world. He has given us his authority to resist the devil and his evil influence. We have been empowered to heal the sick, raise the dead, drive out demons, and reveal the light of his gospel in dark places.

Lie #2: "God is sovereign"

My bankrupt friend wrote off his loss saying, "God is sovereign." In other words, it was God's divine and mysterious will for him to lose all his money. He was not saying "God is king" — no argument there. He was saying, "Everything that happens is the Lord's will." This is simply not true. It was not God's will for Adam to eat from the forbidden tree (Genesis 2:17), yet Adam ate. God is not willing that any perish (2 Peter 3:9), yet people perish. God commands all people everywhere to repent (Acts 17:30), yet many don't.

You don't have to read more than three chapters into the Bible to realize that Almighty God, the Supreme Ruler of all, does not always get what he wants. How is this possible? This verse explains it:

> The highest heavens belong to the Lord, but the earth he has given to mankind. (Psalm 115:16)

God is Lord of the universe but we are little lords of our own little worlds. This is God's gift to us—the freedom to choose how we live. The cost of this gift is that we can make choices contrary to God's will.

The "God is sovereign" mantra is trotted out every time something bad happens but it's just not true. The word sovereign is not even in the Bible!

The truth is that God is *not* sovereign in the sense that he always gets what he wants. His will is *not* always done. Why do you think Jesus taught us to pray, "Let your will be done on earth as it is in heaven"?

But the good news is that God will write the final chapter of human history and for those who trust him all things will work out for good.

Lie #3: "God could've stopped this from happening but didn't"

A boy takes a loaded gun to school and God doesn't stop him. An earthquake flattens a city and God does nothing. What kind of God is this?!

The "God could've stopped this but didn't" chestnut is another way of saying, "This bad thing is God's fault. He *allowed* it to happen."

Like the other two lies we've looked at, there's a measure of truth behind this. Everything that happens happens because God gave us the freedom to do what we like, even the freedom to hate and kill each other and then blame him for what we did. Of course, we look like fools when we do this. We look like Adam who blamed God for giving him a woman who led him into sin (Genesis 3:12).

We are masters at playing the blame game. When something bad happens we blame our genes, our parents, our spouses, our kids. We blame the government, the system, immigrants, terrorists, so we might as well go the whole way and blame God. "I got sick. God allowed this to happen. God is at fault."

Jesus, on the other hand, never blamed anyone. He just took responsibility for other people's messes and fixed them.

Believe the lie that God is behind everything that happens and you'll end up in the ash heap of life licking your wounds and examining your navel like a perplexed Job. You'll bend over whenever the devil wants to kick you. Who wants to live like that?

The truth is God doesn't always stop bad things from happening. The good news is that sometimes you can. You can bring the weight of his purposes to bear on your circumstances by trusting him. You can

walk through the valley of the shadow of death
without fear knowing that he is with you.

A simple test

Which of the following Jesuses is found the Bible?

- Jesus #1 sat around powerless, making excuses
  and doing nothing to help those who had been
  made sick by God
- Jesus #2 went around in the power of the Spirit
  doing good and healing all who were oppressed
  by the devil

Hopefully you know the second Jesus is true (see Acts
10:38). Yet sometimes we who claim to follow Christ
look more like the first Jesus. We're not walking in
the power of the spirit and we're not healing the sick.
Instead we're making excuses like, "God is in control.
It's his fault, not ours."

I don't write this to condemn you but to make you
angry at Satan's lies. James said "resist the devil and
he will flee from you." It's that simple. We resist, he
flees. But we won't resist if we think God is doing the
devil's work and making us sick, killing our kids, and
robbing us blind.

God is not making you sick and poor! He is not
the reason you lost your money, your job, your
marriage, or your kids. These are the tragedies of a
world cursed by Adam's sin. But the good news is
that one greater than Adam has come and given you

authority to proclaim the good news of his kingship to all creation.

Are you sick? Talk to your sickness about Jesus by whose stripes you are healed (1 Peter 2:24).

Are you poor? Talk to your bank account about your rich King who became poor so that through his poverty you might become rich (2 Corinthians 8:9).

Have you been robbed, discouraged, and beaten by life? Then be like David and strengthen yourself in the Lord your mighty God (1 Samuel 30:6).

Did Jesus come to help us understand why God never lifts a finger to help? No. Jesus came to destroy the works of the devil (1 John 3:8). In his name go and do likewise.

A word after

This article made people angry for two reasons. Some were angry because I said God isn't responsible for all the bad stuff that happens, and others were angry because they had been led to believe that he is.

I shouldn't be surprised that this article made people angry. I was angry when I wrote it. I was angry when I heard the awful stuff coming from my friend's mouth. Of course, I wasn't angry at him. I was angry at the devil who dares to keeps God's children bound with such awful lies.

I guess that's the right sort of anger to have — anger at those things that hurt people. If so, then I was pleased to hear from a reader called Gigi:

> This article made me angry! I am angry at Satan's lies which sadly are still being propagated by a number of churches. I am angry that from time to time I still catch myself believing these lies. Jesus wants us to have life and that's the absolute truth!

I couldn't have said it better.

In the article I said that the word sovereign is not in the Bible. However, it does appear in the New International Version almost 300 times since the NIV translators use "sovereign Lord" where others have "Lord God." However, this interpretation of sovereign, meaning "God as supreme ruler," differs from the modern usage which means "God is in control and therefore responsible for all the bad stuff that happens." As we have seen, this interpretation is unbiblical and very bad news.

God is not responsible for all that happens to you, but he is redemptive. He takes the messes of our lives and works them into something good. This is especially true for those who respond to his love and call (Romans 8:28).

Incidentally, one of the worst words in the Christian vernacular must surely be the word allowed, as in God allowed this bad thing to happen. That makes it sound like God gave tacit permission to the thief, the rapist, and the murderer. But if God allowed thieves to steal, they wouldn't be thieves, would they?

5. What about Hebrews 10:26?

I get asked more questions on Hebrews 10:26 than any other verse in the Bible. Evidently, this is a verse that troubles many people:

> If we deliberately keep on sinning after we have received the knowledge of the truth, no sacrifice for sins is left (Hebrews 10:26)

Let's take a quick survey. Put your hand up if you have lived a sinless life. Hmm. I don't see any hands. I have been saved for decades and, to be completely honest with you, I cannot say my performance has been flawless throughout that period. I'm pretty sure I sinned this one time back in 1987...

Ha! It's easy for me to make jokes. I've been set free. I no longer mine at the pits of religion with condemnation. I'm drawing from the wells of salvation with joy.

All jokes aside, Hebrews 10:26 is an oft-abused scripture. If you wanted to use this verse to scare people, there are a couple of angles you could take:

1. You could use this verse to present a "balanced" view of God, like this: "He is a God of grace *and* he is a God of judgment. You need to love him *and* fear him for he's a God of vengeance and a consuming fire. It is a dreadful thing to fall into the hands of the living God."

2. You could also use this verse to preach works: "You will be judged according to the light of your revelation and those who have received the knowledge of the truth will be held to the highest standard. It's time for judgment to begin in the house of God. If you fall away it is impossible to be brought back to repentance!"

What's the problem with these messages? If you listen to the first one you're going to come away thinking that God is schizophrenic, at war with his own good nature. He loves you, but he doesn't. It's unconditional love, with conditions. And if you listen to the second you'll either end up a religious fraud or a nervous wreck. You may even wish that you had never heard the gospel because ignorance is bliss.

The tricky part with these false messages is that they are composed of true statements. Our God *is* a consuming fire. But any message that tells you that God is double-minded or that the good news is bad news ought to be rejected. You know that, right? Good. So how do we read Hebrews 10:26?

Trampling the Son of God under foot

A key to unpacking this scripture is to recall the audience. Hebrews was written for Hebrews. It was written for those who had grown up with the "elementary teachings" of the old covenant. In other words, it's an *informed* audience. They know about the law, sacrifices, and high priests. But what they may not appreciate is that the law was only "a shadow of the good things to come." The law points to the true high priest Jesus and his eternally perfect sacrifice.

Hebrews was written to reveal Christ and his work so that we may "enter through the new and living way," "go on to maturity," and "draw near to God" (Hebrews 6:1, 10:20,22). That last one is key. How do I know the two sermonettes above are nonsense? Because neither will inspire you to draw near to God. Indeed, they will have the opposite effect.

Hebrews 10:26 describes those who have received the knowledge of the truth (i.e., they have heard the gospel) but they have rejected it. The author compares those who reject grace with those who reject law:

> Anyone who rejected the law of Moses died without mercy on the testimony of two or three witnesses. How much more severely do you think someone deserves to be punished who has trampled the Son of God underfoot, who has treated as an unholy thing the blood of the covenant that sanctified them, and who has insulted the Spirit of grace? (Hebrews 10:28–29)

This passage isn't describing someone who has embraced Jesus but someone who has spurned him.

Think of Judas who spent time in the company of the Lord. He saw grace and truth in the flesh. Yet Judas never saw Jesus as anything other than a teacher. Calling Jesus "Rabbi," as Judas does in Matthew 26:25, is a bit like calling the President "Mister," only more so. It's not just insulting, it's unbelief.

Jesus gave his life for Judas but Judas wasn't interested. He preferred his own sinful life of greed and betrayal. I am sure Judas had many opportunities to repent and put his faith in Jesus, but he never did. He rejected the grace of God that could empower him to say no to sin.

Jesus died for Judas, what more could he do? There is nothing. There is no more sacrifice for sins other than the one Jesus provided. To reject Jesus as Lord is to trample the Son of God underfoot and treat the blood of the covenant as unholy.

How do you insult the Spirit of grace?

If you gave me a brand-new car out of the generosity of your heart, but I insisted on paying for it, you would be insulted. Similarly, we insult the Spirit of grace by trying to pay for what God has freely given us. We may call it "proving our salvation" or "appropriating what God has given" but it's all unbelief. It is like saying, "I need to finish what Christ began."

The wrong way to read Hebrews is to think that God is judging us on our performance. Over and over again Hebrews tells us that it is Jesus and *his* performance that matters. It is *his* sacrifice that made us holy and perfect forever (Hebrews 10:10,14).

How can we interpret Hebrews 10:26 as a warning against sin when Hebrews 9:26 says Christ appeared once for all "to do away with sin by the sacrifice of himself"?

Is it a finished work or isn't it?

If God chooses to remember our sins no more (see Hebrews 8:12, 10:17), what business is it of ours to remind him? Doing so insults the Son of Grace who bore our sins and the Spirit of Grace who remembers them no more.

The warning of Hebrews

The main warning of Hebrews is not in regard to sin but unbelief:

> So we see that they were not able to enter, because of their unbelief. (Hebrews 3:19)

The Hebrews of Moses' day never entered God's rest because they hardened their hearts to his voice. In the New Testament era, many Jews were doing the same thing. They had received the knowledge of truth, they had heard the gospel of grace, but they rejected it.

The author of Hebrews writes to stir up faith. Without it we cannot please God. With it we can come boldly to the throne of grace.

> But we do not belong to those who shrink back
> and are destroyed, but to those who have faith
> and are saved. (Hebrews 10:39)

Some people hear the good news of God's grace and shrink back. They cannot believe it. "It's too good to be true," they say. "I'd better save myself by doing works."

Do you see the danger? You cannot save yourself. You cannot elevate yourself to co-savior with Christ. This is why sermons that put the emphasis on you and your performance are so dangerous.

Don't buy into any message that purports to give you a list of keys or steps that will help you achieve/accomplish/appropriate what you already have. It is impossible for the blood of bulls and the sweat of men to take away sins and it is faithless to strive for what you already have (which is every good thing in Christ Jesus).

According to Hebrews there are only two kinds of people; those who don't enter because of unbelief and those who believe and are saved. Sin is not the variable; faith is. Where does faith come from? Jesus! He is the Author and Perfecter of our faith (Hebrews 12:2). Fix your eyes on him.

A word after

Apparently I didn't do a very good job with this one because a reader said, "I don't get it. Can you explain this passage once more?" Here's the short version: If we will not be satisfied and rest in the finished work of the cross, then nothing can save us, for there is no other sacrifice for sins. And here's the shorter version: There's no Plan B. It's Jesus or nothing.

6. Don't Listen to Job's Friends

A few days ago a house on the Sunshine Coast in Australia was destroyed in a fire started by faulty Christmas lights. A family of five were sleeping inside but only the father managed to escape the flames. The neighbors found him in the driveway "burnt from head to toe" and screaming in pain. There is some speculation that his wife might have been able to save herself but she stayed with her children, two of whom were disabled.

As a father, my heart breaks for this man. When he wakes up in hospital he will learn the awful news that he has lost his entire family.

I wish I could go to that man in the burn unit and say something to ease his pain, but I don't know what I would say. However, I know what I *wouldn't* say:

> Endure hardship as discipline; God is treating you as his children. For what children are not disciplined by their father? (Hebrews 12:7)

If that seems out of left field, it's because I have just read something that has my blood boiling. There is steam coming out of my ears. Here's a paraphrase: "You should view every hardship in life as God's loving discipline. God is sovereign and everything that happens to you, good or bad, is for your good. Indeed, it is proof of his love for the Lord disciplines those he loves."

Apparently this is meant to be comforting. Maybe you just lost your wife and kids in a house-fire but be comforted for God did it. Why? Because he loves you.

And we wonder why the lost aren't embracing us as bearers of the good news!

Job 2.0

Some time ago I wrote that God was not responsible for Job's loss no matter what Job 1:21 says. I still get emails on a regular basis that say, "How dare you contradict the Bible? How dare you say that God is not the author of evil?" How can I say it? Because Jesus said it:

> The thief comes only to steal and kill and destroy; I have come that they may have life, and have it to the full. (John 10:10)

Isn't it strange that most Christians would hesitate to tell the burned man that his family and home were destroyed by the devil – "you can't blame Satan for everything" – yet there are some who are quick to point the finger at our loving Father? "God did it." But why would God kill little children in their sleep? "Who can say? God is mysterious."

Forgive me for ranting, but this is insane! It is exactly this sort of madness that makes the church look like a home for whackos. This kind of thinking dishonors the Lord, and it keeps us passive when we should be taking a stand and fighting back. Instead of resisting the devil so that he flees, we submit to the devil and say, "The Lord is disciplining us. Oh we're so loved!"

And this is why I am writing. There is a time for enduring hardship and there is a time for resisting the devil and you need to know the difference.

As usual, Jesus shows the way. He did not consider sickness a hardship to be endured — he resisted it. Neither did he consider demonic oppression a hardship to be endured — he resisted it. At times he even resisted death by raising a little girl and a dead man. He spoke to storms and said we would speak to mountains. Jesus did all these things to show us how the Father responds to the devil's work. And yes, I have no problem attributing sickness to the devil, because the Bible does:

> You know... how God anointed Jesus of Nazareth with the Holy Spirit and power, and how he went around doing good and healing all who were under the power of the devil, because God was with him. (Act 10:37–38)

I said I didn't know what I would say to the man in the burn unit, but Jesus would know. He would reveal the "God of all comfort who comforts us in all of our troubles" (2 Corinthians 1:3–4).

If I was in a position to visit that man I would trust the Holy Spirit to show me what to say and do.

Sadly, accidents are a fact of life and sometimes children die. I cannot imagine the pain of that loss, but I believe there's healing for everything. You want to talk about the mystery of God? Then marvel at how he is able to bring good even out of the most awful of circumstances.

Arise shine!

The bad news of dead religion has reduced Christians to commentators on the sidelines of life. If something good happens, we congratulate each other for sowing into kingdom principles. But if something bad happens, we say the Lord did it because he loves us. This is a nauseating and useless theology. Live this way and you will never display the manifold wisdom of God to rulers and authorities in heavenly realms (Ephesians 3:10).

I don't normally write in reaction to things like this but I had to vent. I'm heartbroken for the man in the burn unit and I'm heartbroken over a church that gets its theology from Job's friends.

I began by paraphrasing some bad writing ("Hardship is proof that God loves you"). I'm going to finish by paraphrasing something that's pure gold. You can decide which you prefer.

See Jesus! See the finished work of the cross! Your light has come and the glory of the Lord rises upon you. You may have problems and hardships and yes thick darkness is over the peoples. But the Lord rises upon you and his glory appears over you. Those mountains are coming down! You may be a worm, little Jacob, but God himself will help you. He will make you into a threshing sledge with many teeth. You will thresh the mountains and crush them, and reduce the hills to chaff. (Isaiah 41:13–14, 60:1–2, my paraphrase)

Don't listen to Job's friends. Listen to Isaiah! It's not about the mountains we face but whether we will turn to God who is greater than every peak, every trial, and every hardship that comes our way.

A word after

Here's a tip every writer should know: you live and die on your headlines. As the copyeditor says, "Headlines are the most important thing you'll ever write."

The article above originally was published with a lousy title and nobody read it. (It also came out on a New Year's Eve which didn't help.) By any measure it was not one of E2R's Greatest Hits.

But this is my book and I think it needs to be read, so here it is. Did you like it?

Actually, a lady called Janet did read it and she responded with an absolute gem of a comment. She wrote, "God cannot give you what he does not have and he doesn't have sickness and disease." Janet must be a copywriter, for she said in sixteen words what I've been trying to say for years.

7. Does God Scourge Us?

What comes to mind when you think of God? Perhaps you think he is distant, aloof, angry, even terrifying. Maybe you see him with a whip in his hands:

> For whom the Lord loves he chastens, and scourges every son whom he receives. (Hebrews 12:6, NKJV)

Yet your heavenly Father is not like this. He is loving, gracious, and kind. Jesus said he was about his Father's business and that business is not the scourging business but the adoption business. God loves you and wants to spend eternity with you.

So how does scourging fit into this picture? It doesn't. It sticks out like a cobra in a kindergarten. It shouldn't be there. Yet there it is, in black and white in Hebrews 12. So does God scourge his kids or doesn't he?

What is scourging?

In our era of first-world problems, you may not be acquainted with the horrors of scourging. But those who lived in New Testament times knew at least two types of scourging.

First, there was Jewish scourging which involved the application of a leather whip to your shoulders

ESCAPE TO REALITY – GREATEST HITS VOL. 4

and chest. This form of scourging was limited by Jewish law to 40 stripes. This is why the Jews called it the "forty lashes minus one" — they didn't want to risk breaking the law by miscounting so they deliberately reduced the maximum number of lashes to 39! The law also said that the actual number of lashes was supposed to be commensurate with the crime. However, Paul got the "forty minus one" on at least five occasions even though he broke no law (2 Corinthians 11:24).

Then there was Roman scourging which was worse. It was typically applied to criminals before execution and there was no limit to the number of strokes. In fact, if you wanted to kill a man at the whipping post, you could do it with a vicious tool called the flagellum. Since there may be children reading this, I won't describe what the Roman whip could do to a body of flesh and blood, but if you have seen *The Passion* movie, you will know.

Regardless of whether you got the Jewish whip or the Roman one, scourging was torture. Today it's not the sort of thing civilized societies would inflict even on the worst criminals. Yet apparently God does it to his kids.

Does God really scourge us?

"The Lord scourges every son he receives." The original Greek word is the same word that describes what Pilate had done to Jesus (John 19:1). So if you

need a mental picture of God's scourging, you'll be
wanting the Roman flagellum with the bits of metal
in the thongs and the little hooks called scorpions at
the end.

If this troubles you, I'm glad. It means you have a
brain. It means you are struggling to reconcile a good
God with an evil whip. I'm here to tell you that our
heavenly Father never, ever, *ever* scourges his kids.
Not ever! But before I give you my reasons, I have to
be honest and admit that every single commentator
I've read says that he does. They all say stuff like this:

> Scourging is God-ordained suffering. In response
> to sin he whips us using trials and tribulations
> which he ordains to mortify the flesh and nurture
> faith. Scourging is not a one-off event, but some-
> thing to be expected in the lives of his children.

In other words, God scourges us *repeatedly*. Isn't that
wonderful? Sheesh. No wonder the lost aren't run-
ning into church when we're preaching stuff like that.

It's a misquote

Look in the margin notes of your Bible and you will
see that Hebrews 12:6 is quoting Proverbs 3:11–12. It's
a direct quote copied from the Old Testament and
pasted into the New. Let's put the original Proverb
and the Hebrews version side by side and see if you
can spot any differences:

My son, do not despise the chastening of the Lord,
Nor detest his correction;
For whom the Lord loves he corrects,
Just as a father the son in whom he delights.
~Original quote from Proverbs 3:11–12 (NKJV)

My son, do not despise the chastening of the Lord,
Nor be discouraged when you are rebuked by
    him
For whom the Lord loves he chastens,
And scourges every son whom he receives
~As reproduced in Hebrews 12:5–6 (NKJV)

The first three lines of the original Proverb are faithfully reproduced in Hebrews 12. But look at the last line and you will see that the copy is nothing like the original. The original quote has been changed. Am I saying the Bible is wrong? Not at all. My best guess is the problem was introduced during translation. (I'll share some thoughts about this in my Word After.)

Why you can be sure God does not scourge us

In the Bible, the word for scourge appears in six other places. On each occasion it is associated with punishment inflicted by the unjust upon the just, such as Jesus or those who follow him.[3] Given this context, to

---

[3] If you're interested, here are the scripture references: Matthew 10:17, 20:19, 23:34, Mark 10:34, Luke 18:32, and John 19:1.

say that God scourges his sons is tantamount to saying that a just God acts unjustly, which he doesn't.

In Biblical times, scourging was reserved for slaves and criminals, not sons and citizens. Paul was unjustly scourged yet he never said, "I was scourged for my good." Instead, he resisted scourging (see Acts 22:25), as should every free man and woman.

Hebrews 12 says God disciplines or trains us as a father. I don't know any father, good or bad, who scourges his kids the way the Romans scourged Jesus. It's a metaphor that doesn't work at any level. God doesn't train us with whips. He nurtures us (see Ephesians 6:4).

However, there was one father in the Bible who was known for using whips and rods, and that was Solomon. We know he used the rod of correction because he tells us in Proverbs 13:24. Solomon evidently had old-school views regarding corporal punishment, yet even he didn't whip his sons. He said whips were for horses (Proverbs 26:3).

I've heard people say they won't respond unless God whips them. That's like saying, "I'm as dumb as a horse." Renew your mind. You are not a horse! You are a beloved child of God.

Others say "discipline implies punishment." Not in the new covenant it doesn't (see Isaiah 53:5). Discipline implies *discipling*.

Jesus met plenty of people in need of correction and discipline. How many of these people did he scourge? How many did he afflict with pain, sickness, trials, or suffering? None. If Jesus was ever going to whip someone, he might've whipped the Pharisees, but he didn't.

The suggestion that God scourges his kids with a flagellum is slanderous, ludicrous, and inconsistent. I am convinced that the author of Hebrews had a profound revelation of God with-no-whip. The picture he paints is of a good God sitting on a throne of grace who offers us grace and mercy in our time of need (Hebrews 4:16). When we go astray God does not come after us with a whip, but he deals with us gently as a loving father deals with his sons (Hebrews 5:2).

What is Hebrews really saying?

In my view, the Hebrew author of the epistle to the Hebrews meant to say something like what we see in the Hebrew proverb, namely:

> For whom the Lord loves he *disciples* (he trains, instructs and nurtures), just as a father the son in whom he delights. (Hebrews 12:6, my paraphrase)

This may be a better translation than the one we have in our English Bible because it satisfies three tests: (1) It is consistent with the revelation of God the Father given to us through Jesus the Son, (2) it is consistent with many other scriptures indicating that God delights in his children and that he cares enough to train and disciple us, and (3) it fits the encouraging context of Hebrews 12.

A word after

It is cavalier of me to take a scripture I cannot reconcile with the gospel and say, "It was translated wrong." Goodness, why don't I just do that with every tough scripture?

But hand on heart, this is the only time I have done this and I believe I have solid Biblical grounds for doing so. If Hebrews 10:26 is a quote from the Old Testament, then it's an inaccurate one, as anyone can see. That alone should give us pause. We might then ask, "Which is the best translation of the Bible?" Easy question. Jesus is! The Living Word is the best translation of the written word.

Can you imagine Jesus scourging those he loves? Can you see him wrapping a flagellum around the backs of one of his disciples? Of course not. It's preposterous! Then why do we think the Father would do it? As a wise person once said, if it's not true of the Son, it's not true of the Father. (See Hebrews 1:3 if that makes no sense.)

"Wait a second, Paul. Didn't Jesus make a whip of cords and drive the money-changers out of the temple?" Actually he drove out the *animals*. "He made a whip out of cords, and drove all from the temple courts, both sheep and cattle" (John 2:15a).

Jesus was very smart. He knew that you don't need a whip to clear out merchants and money-changers. A herd of stampeding oxen will do the job nicely.

8. Fear and Trembling

> Therefore, my dear friends, as you have always obeyed — not only in my presence, but now much more in my absence — continue to work out your salvation with fear and trembling… (Philippians 2:12)

This is a verse that works preachers love to quote. They use it to say that salvation is something to work for and that we must tip-toe fearfully through life lest we upset a wrathful God. It sounds spiritual, but it's an anti-Christ message that insults the Spirit of grace.

I've said it before and I'll say it again: Jesus did it all! His work was perfectly perfect and completely complete. Because of his sacrifice you have been made perfect forever. As he is, so are you in this world. Rest in him.

Work out your own salvation…

What does it mean to work out your salvation? Salvation literally means deliverance, preservation, safety, as well as salvation. It is a picture of a new life where all your needs — your need for forgiveness, deliverance, healing, provision — are supplied according to his riches in glory by Christ Jesus (Philippians 4:19).

On the cross Jesus provided for your complete salvation, healing, and deliverance. If your old way of life was characterized by poverty, curses, and never enough, then your new life in Christ is one of abundance, blessings and more than enough.

"But Paul, I don't see it. I'm not healthy. I'm not prospering. I'm not overcoming." Then *work out* in faith the good gift that God has placed within you. In him you lack nothing.

> Praise be to the God and Father of our Lord Jesus Christ, who has blessed us in the heavenly realms with *every spiritual blessing* in Christ. (Ephesians 1:3, emphasis added)

God has already blessed us with every blessing in Christ. If you have Christ, you have everything you'll ever need. The blessings are spiritual in origin until we work them out. For instance, his forgiveness is a done deal, but you need to believe it to live free from guilt and condemnation.

But what about the second part of the verse?

...with fear and trembling

I used to think this phrase was describing our proper state before God, and that we should be afraid and tremble because even after a lifetime of service God might judge that we haven't done enough for him. Thank God for the cross! God isn't looking at me and my performance but Jesus and his. I no longer fear judgment because my sin has been carried away and I am now clothed with Christ.

In this passage, Paul is not talking about judgment at all, but the outworking of our salvation. Why is fear and trembling involved? Because sometimes trusting God can be scary!

The other day I saw on YouTube a paralyzed lady get out of a wheelchair and take her first tentative steps in 23 years. She was trembling when she did it. It happened in a church and we can only imagine what was going through her mind. What if she fell on her face in front of hundreds of people? Her wheelchair was her comfort zone, but in faith she faced her fears and received a miracle.

Faith is risky!

Faith is often accompanied by fear and trembling. How do you think Abraham felt as he was about to plunge the knife into Isaac? We know that Abraham was fully persuaded that God would raise the dead — that's faith — but he would not have been human if he hadn't trembled.

And do you think Rahab was in a joyful mood when she welcomed the spies of Israel into her home? Her faith meant a death sentence if the soldiers of Jericho discovered her treason.

What about Daniel in the lions' den, or David facing the giant, or Moses standing up to Pharaoh? Is it so hard to imagine that these heroes of faith acted with fear and trembling?

Faith means putting something on the line. It might be your comfort, your reputation, your family, your funds, even your life—but faith usually means something is risked.

You may want to run away

My favorite line in the film *Avatar* is "Run! Definitely run!" Apparently this is the proper thing to do when you meet one of Pandora's more aggressive beasts. Fear often manifests as a desire to run away. Indeed, the words fear and flight are connected in the Greek language. So our choice is often one of faith or flight. I know something about that.

Years ago, when it became apparent that Camilla and I were going to be handed the leadership of a church, I told her "pack your bags, we're leaving." I didn't want to be a pastor. I feared failure. Paul felt the same way about going to Corinth:

> And so it was with me, brothers and sisters. When I came to you, I did not come with eloquence or human wisdom… I came to you in weakness with great fear and trembling. (1 Corinthians 2:1a,3)

Paul was a mighty man of faith, yet he went to Corinth "with fear and great trembling." A part of him didn't want to go. In fact, Paul was so fearful that

God had to step in and say "do not be afraid" (Acts 18:9).

There's grace for us here. Paul is saying, "It's not wrong to be fearful." But in the presence of these feelings, work out your salvation anyway. Take the faith-risk, because you will be blessed if you do.

But you will be blessed if you stay

A preacher of works will use Philippians 2:12 to get you to perform out of fear. But there is a big difference between works done in fear and works done in faith. In fear we may *work for God*, but in faith we get to do the *work of God*. In this passage Paul is talking about the second kind of work:

> … it is God who works in you to will and to act in order to fulfill his good purpose. (Philippians 2:13)

If God is the one working, what part do we play? We are the ones who decide who gets to see the King! God can do whatever he wants, but in his wisdom he has chosen to reveal himself through the faith of his saints. We preach and his signs and wonders follow. We lay hands on the sick and his healing is released. So what happens if we don't preach or lay hands on the sick?

Paul didn't want to go to Corinth, but he went anyway. Despite fear and trembling he preached

Christ crucified and the result was that many Corinthians believed and were baptized (Acts 18:8).

Jonah didn't want to preach in Nineveh, but he did and an entire city was saved. Both Jonah and Paul took faith-risks despite their fears. As a result, the kingdom of God came to two cities and thousands were saved.

Fear and trembling are normal. What you do with fear is the thing. We can live afraid and see nothing change, or we can face our fears and see the kingdom come.

Working out our salvation means that at some point we're going to have to get out of the boat and take a risk. God won't punish us if we hold back—this has nothing to do with punishment. But we will be blessed, and the nations will be blessed through us, when we reveal Jesus.

A word after

I've given you a few examples of people who stepped out in faith with fear and trembling (Abraham, Rahab, Paul, Jonah), but one reader suggested another:

> At once Jesus realized that power had gone out from him. He turned around in the crowd and asked, "Who touched my clothes?" … Then the woman, knowing what had happened to her, came and fell at his feet and, *trembling with fear*,

told him the whole truth. (Mark 5:30,33, emphasis added)

Two thousand years later we marvel at this woman's faith, but let's not forget her fear and trembling. Under law, this woman was considered unclean (Leviticus 15:25), and as such she was forbidden to touch others. Yet here in the press of the crowd she touched everybody, risking their ire. But while she came "trembling with fear," she left in peace and healed from her suffering. What a difference faith makes!

You may be wondering what happened in my own story, the one where I told Camilla to pack her bags because I didn't want to be left with a church. Although the temptation to run away was strong, we stayed for ten wonderful years. I learned so much during that time that if we had run away then, I doubt I would be writing to you now.

9. Three Reasons Why I Don't Preach Turn from Sin

I've heard people complain that grace preachers don't emphasize repentance sufficiently. It's true. I hardly emphasize it at all. But then neither did the Apostle John. Search his gospel and epistles and you will not find the word repentance anywhere. I guess John must've been a grace preacher.

Here's something that may fry your mind: Repentance is one of the most important things you'll ever do—you need to repent!—but you won't get people to repent by preaching on it. "How can you say such heresy Paul?" I'll answer that question in a moment. But first, which of the following is the best definition of repentance:

1. Repentance means turning from sin
2. Repentance means changing your mind

Repentance, like football, means different things to different people. Those under law define repentance as turning from sin. But when Jesus came preaching "repent and believe the good news," he meant "change the way you think about God."

In the old covenant, sinners repented by bringing a sacrifice of penance and confessing their sins (Numbers 5:7). But in the new we bring a sacrifice of praise and confess his name (Hebrews 13:15).

Under the old, you had to deal with your sin. But in the new, Jesus has done it all. Our part is to quit trusting in dead works, believe the good news, and say thank you Jesus!

Yet some people just can't see the cross for their sins.

No matter how much I tell them about God's goodness, they tell me I'm under-selling repentance. What they really mean is, "Paul you're not telling people to turn from their sin."

In many churches this is exactly the message you will hear. "God is holy and he won't accept you unless you turn from sin."

It's sold as a message of repentance and it appeals to our sense of right and wrong, but it's dangerous and misleading for it promotes dead works and can keep you from coming to Jesus.

It may seem like I'm splitting hairs, but what you think of when you hear the word repent is the difference between life and death.

Does your repenting cause you to think of your badness or God's goodness? Does it lead you to dwell on your sins or his Son?

As I say, repentance is essential. We all need to repent and repentance ought to be our daily lifestyle. But there are at least three good reasons why you should reject any message that defines repentance as turning from sin:

1. Preaching "turn from sin" puts people under law

"Turn from sin or you're not saved." This is pure law. It's prescribing sin-rejection as a means for salvation. This law-based message sounds good but it actually leaves listeners worse off because it empowers the sin that enslaves while scorning the grace of God that might otherwise save us (see 1 Corinthians 15:56).

The righteousness that God offers is not purchased by your turning performance. The free gift of righteousness comes by faith from first to last.

2. Preaching "turn from sin" doesn't actually lead people to salvation

Suppose I call you up and give you an invitation to come to my house. You've never been here before so you need directions. There are two ways I could direct you. I could give you my address and provide an accurate picture of where I live. Or I could say, "Flee from your house—just drive as fast as possible and don't look back." Do you see the difference?

In both cases you're going to leave your house, that's guaranteed. But only by trusting my directions will you actually arrive at my house.

Repentance is just like that. It's not fleeing from sin like a Pharisee; it's turning to God in faith. In both cases you will leave your sin. But only by trusting God will you actually arrive someplace better than where you started.

To get people to repent (change their minds) Jesus preached the good news of the kingdom. He painted a picture of where God wanted them to be (with him) and he gave them clear directions on how to get there (turn to God in faith). Jesus never preached "turn from sin." He preached the gospel and the result was people turned from sin.

3. We're called to preach the gospel, not "turn from sin"

Repentance is one of the most important things you'll ever do but you'll never do it without a good reason. Jesus is the good reason! Your sin is an inferior reason.

Jesus loves you, he died for you and offers you his righteousness. *Do you believe it?*

Faith and repentance are two sides of the same coin. Repentance, like faith, is a positive response to something God has done.

In his gospel John never mentions repentance directly, yet he talks about believing again and again. He wrote his book so "that you may believe that Jesus is the Christ, the Son of God, and that by believing you may have life in his name" (John 20:31). The key to life is not in turning from sin but trusting in Jesus. This is the true meaning of repentance.

Paul said repentance comes from hearing about the goodness of God (see Romans 2:4). You want people to repent? Then preach the gospel that reveals the goodness of a good God: Jesus has done it all!

A word after

Oh boy, what a hornet's nest this article proved to be! It's probably the most controversial thing I've written.

Some complained that I am opposed to repenttance. (I am not. I'm 100 percent for it!) Others said I was preaching universal salvation. (I'm not sure how since I'm encouraging people to turn to God and believe in Jesus.) And a few called me a heretic. (It wouldn't be the first time.)

But what no one did was dispute my claim that preaching "turn from sin" puts people under law and distracts us from preaching the gospel. On this we are all agreed. (I think.) So what's the problem? Why the fuss?

The problem is there has been such a huge emphasis on old covenant repentance (turn from sin), that we have gotten used to it. It seems right that we should turn from sin (we should!) and that if we want more people to turn from sin we should tell them to do it (we shouldn't!). I'm not questioning the logic. I'm just saying it doesn't work. It never has.

I'm with Spurgeon who said, "Repentance will not make you see Christ; but to see Christ will give you repentance."[4] You want people to repent? Then reveal Christ. Preach the gospel of Jesus.

---

[4] This is from Spurgeon's book *All of Grace*, which is one of the best books on grace you'll ever read. Since it has long been out of copyright, you can get PDF copies of it for free off the web. Google it.

10. What is Biblical Correction?

What you look through determines what you see. Read the Bible through the fractured lens of human wisdom and you will think the secret to life is doing right and avoiding wrong. You'll go to God with an attitude of, "Just tell me what to do and I'll do it." But this is eating from the wrong tree. It leads to independence instead of faith.

Life is not about doing right and avoiding wrong. Nor is it about sinning versus non-sinning. That's a language your Father doesn't speak. The issue isn't good versus evil, but life versus death. And this issue is clearly seen when dealing with sin.

How does God respond when I sin?

Elsewhere I have said that the Holy Spirit never convicts us of our sins. Instead, the Holy Spirit brings about a life-saving correction.[5]

"But Paul, isn't that just two ways of saying the same thing? What's the difference?"

The difference is this: If you think the Holy Spirit convicts you *because of your sin* or corrects you *because of your sin*, you've missed the cross. You're looking backwards instead of forwards and down instead of up.

---

[5] See chapter 4, "Ten myths about the Holy Spirit," in *Grace Classics: Escape to Reality — Greatest Hits, Vol. 2.*

The Holy Spirit isn't your personal sin manager, but your Helper, your Comforter, your Counselor. And in that role he will guide you, correct you, and, if necessary, rebuke or admonish you. He does none of this in reaction to your sin, per se. He does it because he loves and cares for you, and he doesn't want you to wreck your life over some death-dealing decision.

Here's a question to see how well you understand this: What comes to mind when you hear the word *correction*? Do you think of a mistake that needs to be punished? Do you think of the rod of correction and naughty boys in need of a whipping? If you do, God bless you but your thinking is influenced by the old covenant (see Proverbs 22:15).

In the Old Testament the word for correct can mean "to chastise with blows." It's applying the proverbial rod to the seat of learning. In grown-up terms it means plagues and punishment sent in response to sin. At least that's how David saw it:

> Remove your plague from me; I am consumed by the blow of your hand. When with rebukes you correct man for iniquity, you make his beauty melt away like a moth. Surely every man is vapor. (Psalm 39:10–11, NKJV)

Under the old covenant the chastisement of the Lord was sometimes fatal. Get it wrong and you were toast. Thank God for Jesus! Thank God that "the chastisement for our peace was upon *him*" (Isaiah 53:5). Jesus died for our sins so that we don't have to. Because of Jesus we need a new definition of correction.

When I hear the word correction I think of a sailboat heading in a dangerous direction. A course correction needs to be made. The sailboat isn't necessarily sinning or wrong, it's just going the wrong way. We could curse the map or apply the rod of correction to the sat-nav, but what will that accomplish? Far better just to get back on course.

> All scripture is God-breathed and is useful for teaching, rebuking, correcting and training in righteousness… (2 Timothy 3:16)

In the new covenant the word for correction means "a straightening up again." Isn't that wonderful? All is not lost. You are not toast. You can be straightened up again. You may be heading towards the shoals or you may have already hit the shoals and sunk your boat, but the Holy Spirit who raises the dead can still lead you back to the way of life. Your life is not over.

Case study: The Galatians

> You were doing so well until someone made you turn from the truth. (Galatians 5:7, CEV)

The Galatians had started well but they veered off course. They needed to be straightened up again and the Holy Spirit worked through Paul to bring about that needed course correction.

In the Bible correction (gentle warnings) and rebuking (big warnings) are often mentioned together. This is how a loving Father trains his sons — not through sickness or other tribulations and certainly not through blows! The word discipline means discipling or training and God does that primarily by giving us a revelation of his righteousness through the word.

> Preach the word in season, out of season. Reprove (admonish), rebuke (announce those life-saving course corrections), exhort (invite, implore, beseech)… (2 Timothy 4:2, my paraphrase)

Your loving Father is not interested in fault-finding and sin-hunting. However, he loves you too much to stay silent as you sail towards the hidden shoals of life. If you are making poor choices, your Father will definitely seek to bring about a course correction and lead you in the life-giving way of righteousness.

Our problem is we often confuse behavior with identity. When we screw-up we think, "I'm a screw-up." When we sin, we think, "I'm a sinner."

"Not true!" declares the Holy Spirit. "Just as your righteous acts never made you righteous in the first place, your unrighteous acts don't make you un-righteous. Even though you did something dumb, you are still righteous. Now let's go and reveal the life of Jesus into that situation."

When you act out of the false identity of who you used to be (independent and faithless), the Holy Spirit will always seek to remind you of your true identity in Christ. "You are holy and righteous, so act like it."

Love greater than our messes

Look at how Jesus related to the disciples and you will find him doing all the things the Holy Spirit continues to do: guiding, correcting, and rebuking. Not once do you find Jesus saying, "Peter, you're an idjit. Have some cancer, it'll give you character."

And look at how Jesus related to Judas. Did he call him sinner and traitor? No, he called him friend (Matthew 26:50)!

I am so thankful for the gentle correction of the Holy Spirit. When I have gone astray he has consistently brought me back to the way of life. Without the Holy Spirit's help I would have chosen the wrong career and I'd still be preaching the wrong message. Walking by sight I would have sown death left and right. But by the grace of God I am who I am because my Father loves me and he cares about the details of our lives.

And the good news is that if you do make a mess of your life, he still loves you, he still cares for you, and he will never kick you out of his family!

A word after

Here's a multiple choice question to see whether you've got this. When I sin, the Holy Spirit: (a) chastises me with sickness, (b) accuses me of wrong-doing, (c) dumps a bucket of guilt over me, (d) condemns me as a sinner, or (e) none of the above.

If you answered anything other than (e), you need to reread the article. The Holy Spirit will never accuse you, condemn you, make you sick, or send you on a guilt trip. But he will let you know when you are sowing death into your life. Like a lighthouse-keeper he will turn on the light revealing the danger ahead of you.

After reading the article an E2R reader asked me a question. "Where does rebuking fit in? How do we know when we are simply being set back on the right path or rebuked for our poor choice?"

The word which is normally rendered rebuke in our English Bibles means admonish. It is to urge earnestly or issue a strong warning. Don't think of it as God screaming, "Look at what you did!" but "Watch where you are going. Look out for those dangerous shoals!"

The Holy Spirit is not a faultfinder, but he will warn you when the sailboat of your life is heading towards trouble. He does this not to judge or punish you, but because he loves you (see Revelation 3:19). You are the apple of his eye and he doesn't want you to shipwreck your life.

11. Chop Off Your Hand?! Was Jesus Serious?

> If your right hand causes you to sin, cut it off and cast it from you; for it is more profitable for you that one of your members perish, than for your whole body to be cast into hell. (Matthew 5:30, NKJV)

I doubt there's a Christian alive who hasn't wondered about this verse. It's one of those scriptures that causes you to do a double-take. What?! Did Jesus really say that? Was he serious? I'd better ask the pastor.

I'll guess the odds are ten to one you came away thinking that Jesus *wasn't* serious. After all, Jesus is the kindest person there is. He healed people. Surely he doesn't want us to go around maiming ourselves. Then you looked around your church and saw that no one had actually chopped off their hands and so you took comfort in the fact that others thought the same way as you did. There's safety in numbers.

No doubt these words of Jesus are uncomfortable. Maybe you don't think about them much. But Jesus' words are important. Those who don't heed what he says are building on sand.

So let's cut to the chase: was Jesus being figurative or literal when he spoke about chopping off hands?

If you think he was using a figure of speech, how do you know that Jesus wasn't speaking metaphorically all the time? Do we just assume that anytime he said something hard to swallow that he was speaking figuratively?

Or perhaps you think Jesus was being literal. Okay, so what are you going to do about it? Have you done what he said or have you ignored him? It seems our choice is presumption or disobedience or amputation. Is there any other option?

Was Jesus speaking figuratively?

"Jesus is using strong words to convey something about the seriousness of sin," says the theologian. "He's not really preaching self-mutilation but self-denial. What he means to say is we must be sensitive to sin and renounce it and run from it and do whatever it takes to avoid it."

Does this sound familiar to you? It should, for this has been the standard interpretation for most of church history. But there are two fatal flaws with this conclusion. First, it assumes that Jesus was exaggerating and *Jesus never exaggerated*. Preachers sometimes exaggerate to make a point but Jesus always meant what he said and said what he meant. He is Truth personified. It is inconceivable that he would play with words for the crude purpose of ramming home a lesson. When Jesus spoke in parables he did so to conceal truths, not to stretch them (Matthew 13:13). In any case, the passage above is not part of a parable. The context is the Sermon on the Mount and Jesus has just been speaking about anger and lust. His language is plain because the issues are serious. There is nothing metaphorical about his choice of words.

The second flaw with this interpretation is that it suggests we can do stuff to save ourselves from hell. Maybe we don't have to self-amputate, but we can confess, abstain, renounce, run from, and what have you. There's nothing wrong with these things. The error is in thinking we can save ourselves by doing them. No doubt it is better to enter eternal life handi-capped than for your whole body to go to hell. But it does not follow that there is anything you can do to earn eternal life.

Was Jesus speaking literally?

Most people think Jesus was speaking figuratively because they do not believe for a second that he meant what he said. But what if he did? Does it then follow that he actually wants us to chop off our hands? Of course not. We are sanctified by the blood of the Lamb, not our severed limbs. Self-mutilation does nothing to deal with sin for sin is conceived in the heart not the hand (Matthew 5:28). Besides, if you chop one hand off you're left with another. You can still sin!

So what's going on here? Why would Jesus tell us to do something he doesn't really want us to do? He's doing it so we will realize the absurdity of trying to impress God with our acts of self-righteousness. He's preaching the law on steroids, not so that you will try to keep it, but so that you will quit pretending that you are.

It is hard for some to grasp that Jesus could preach both grace and law without confusing the two, but he did. Jesus is the perfect physician. He knows exactly what medicine you need. If you're broken and hurting you'll get grace, but if you're confident of your own self-righteousness you'll get law.

A self-righteous person thinks they can impress God with their religious performance. The only language they understand is law. They say, "All these commands I have kept from my youth, what else do I lack?" And Jesus responds, "Okay, you asked for it, receive some more law."

Why preach the law?

The law is not a standard to live up to, but a mirror that reveals our faults. The law was not given to help you overcome sin, but to help sin overcome you (Romans 7:8–9).

Jesus met people who thought they would be judged righteous if they kept the law. But instead of being silenced by their inability to do so, they lowered the standard making it easier to keep. Jesus didn't like this one bit. In the Sermon on the Mount he took the watered-down law ("You have heard it said") and raised it to a higher level ("but I say unto you"). In other words, he polished the mirror.

Why did Jesus do this? Because some people will never appreciate the good news until they've heard the bad news, which is this:

> Unless your righteousness surpasses that of the Pharisees and the teachers of the law, you will certainly not enter the kingdom of heaven. (Matthew 5:20)

The law is holy, righteous and good, but try to live by it and it will condemn and kill you (2 Corinthians 3:6,9). The purpose of the law is to bring you to the end of yourself and reveal your need for a Savior (Galatians 3:24). If you are self-righteous, you will never appreciate Jesus until the law has plowed the pride out of your heart.

You may say, "I'm a decent person. I've never killed or committed adultery."

"Not good enough," says Jesus. "God knows your heart. If you've entertained murderous or lustful thoughts you've as good as done it. This is a serious business. If you persist in this pathetic course of self-reliance, you had better be prepared to go the whole way even if that means sacrificing an eye and a hand."

And to ram home the point, Jesus says this:

> Be perfect, therefore, as your heavenly Father is perfect. (Matthew 5:48)

God expects perfection and nothing less. If you're not perfect, twenty-four hours a day, seven days a week, you're in serious trouble. That's the bad news. Now here's the good news:

> Do not think that I have come to abolish the law or the prophets; I have not come to abolish them but to fulfill them. (Matthew 5:17)

Jesus fulfilled the righteous requirements of the law on your behalf. You are not perfect, but you have a perfect high priest who is…

> able to save completely those who come to God through him, because he always lives to intercede for them. Such a high priest truly meets our need—one who is holy, blameless, pure, set apart from sinners, exalted above the heavens. (Hebrews 7:25–26)

Why did Jesus preach the law? He did it to prepare our hearts for the good news of God's grace. He did it to show us that we can either trust our own law-keeping performance or his. But what we can't do is dilute the law to some standard lower than perfection and think that impresses God.

Jesus wasn't foolin'

Jesus was born under the law and fulfilled the law to redeem those under the law so that we might receive the full rights of sons (Galatians 4:4-5). Because of what Jesus has done we are no longer under the law but grace (Romans 6:15). The good news is that his righteousness surpasses that of the Pharisees and he offers his righteousness to you as a free gift (Romans 5:17).

To answer the question at the top of this article — was Jesus serious? — yes, he was deadly serious! He was so serious that he suffered and died to redeem you from the curse of the law that he himself preached.

So the next time someone tells you that Jesus was playing with words and that he didn't really mean what he said, don't let them get away with it. Don't let them water down his words to suit their own religious performance. Jesus was not exaggerating to make a point. Neither was he encouraging us to pursue dead works. He was telling us that God expects nothing short of perfection and that he — Jesus — is the only hope we have.

A word after

I said in the article that Jesus never exaggerated. He always said what he meant and meant what he said. So does that mean he wants us to literally hate our mother and father, as he says in Luke 14:26?

I don't think Jesus wants us to hate anybody in the sense that we understand the word. No doubt there have been some who justified their hatred of

others by referring to Christ's words, but in the
Sermon on the Mount Jesus tells us to hate no one
(Matthew 5:43).

So why does Jesus use the word hate when talking about parents? It's such a strong word. We can
get some insight by seeing how Jesus uses the same
word elsewhere:

> No one can serve two masters. Either you will
> hate the one and love the other, or you will be
> devoted to the one and despise the other. You
> cannot serve both God and money. (Matthew 6:24)

To hate is to disregard. Jesus is not saying, "Hate
your parents in the same way that you might hate the
devil." He's saying, "If you are torn between them
and me, disregard them."

I have many friends in Asia for whom this is a
very real choice. Their parents worship Buddha but
they worship Jesus. Some have been kicked out of
their homes because they got water baptized. Their
parents told them, "Get baptized and you're no
longer my son or daughter." They were forced to
choose. It's not that they hate their parents, but they
had to disregard their parents' wishes to follow
Christ.

So Jesus wasn't exaggerating. There is a cost to
this following him and it's one we all pay: "Anyone
who loves their life will lose it, while anyone who
hates their life in this world will keep it for eternal

life" (John 12:25). Jesus is not preaching self-hatred. He's saying, "Have no regard for your life. Do not worry about it. Give it no thought. Seek first my kingdom and my righteousness."

We are kept by that which we cling to, so disregard life, money, and even parents if it comes to it, and cling to Jesus.

12. Fear God Who Can Throw You into Hell?

Do not be afraid of those who kill the body but cannot kill the soul. Rather, be afraid of the One who can destroy both soul and body in hell. (Matthew 10:28)

This verse is a puzzle because of what Jesus says next:

Are not two sparrows sold for a penny? Yet not one of them will fall to the ground outside your Father's care. And even the very hairs of your head are all numbered. So don't be afraid; you are worth more than many sparrows. (Matthew 10:29–31)

Be afraid? Don't be afraid? Which is it? I'm confused. Is Jesus sending a mixed message? Is he trying to scare us? No, he isn't, but there is no doubt that Matthew 10:28 has been used to sow fear and confusion among those whom the Lord loves. This verse has caused anxiety and thoughts like this: "I know God loves me on account of Jesus, but I still need to perform lest he destroy me in hell."

No, no, no! That is not what Jesus is saying. So what's going on in this passage?

Read Matthew 10:28 out of context and you'll end up insecure and anxious. But read this verse in context and you'll end up encouraged and confident of your Father's great love.

The picture in the puzzle

The "be afraid" speech is recorded in two gospels; (1) Matthew 10:28 and (2) Luke 12:5. In Matthew's account Jesus is about to send out the twelve to demonstrate the gospel of the kingdom. In Luke's account Jesus has just rebuked the law experts for taking away the key to knowledge, a reference to the law that reveals sin and our need for Jesus.

So the same speech is recorded twice, in Matthew and Luke, and these two accounts are like a two-piece jigsaw puzzle. A two-piece puzzle is the easiest puzzle there is. You don't need a theology degree to assemble such a simple puzzle. Even a small child can do it, and so can we.

Here's the context: The disciples are about to go and proclaim the gospel and will likely face persecution from the religious leaders and law-lovers. This is what Jesus says to encourage them.

- Go out and reveal the kingdom by healing the sick and driving out demons (Matthew 10:7–8).
- But be on your guard against the yeast of the Pharisees, which is hypocrisy (Luke 12:1). Those guys have the key to knowledge but have not used it to help themselves or others enter the kingdom.
- Since you're going to be sheep among wolves, be as shrewd as snakes and as innocent as doves (Matthew 10:16).

- Know that you will face opposition. You may even be persecuted and tortured (Matthew 10:17).
- If these men have persecuted the head of the house (i.e., me) how much more will they persecute the members of his house (Matthew 10:25).
- But don't be afraid of them because a day is coming when their hypocrisy will be exposed (Matthew 10:26).
- Ha — you want to know who to be afraid of? It's not these clowns who can only hurt your bodies. There is One far scarier than these guys who is able to destroy both body and soul (Matthew 10:28).
- That scary One is your Father who loves you and cares for you (Matthew 10:29).
- As you encounter the opposition of wicked men, remember that Almighty God is *for* you and will vindicate you. So don't be afraid (Matthew 10:31).
- Indeed, don't even worry about what you will eat and wear (Luke 12:22). As you seek the kingdom your loving Father will take care of all your needs (Luke 12:31).
- You who have acknowledged me before men, I will acknowledge before my Father. But those clowns who think they're hot stuff — those law-lovers who have taken away the key to knowledge, have denied me and chosen to remain outside the kingdom — I will deny them before my Father (Matthew 10:32–33).

- So I say again, do not be afraid, little flock, for your Father is pleased to give you the kingdom (Luke 12:32).

See how important it is to read things in context? Jesus isn't threatening his disciples (or anyone) with hell. He is encouraging them. Again and again he says, "Do not be afraid." At first blush this seems unrealistic. How can we not fear given all the trouble and opposition we face when preaching the gospel? "The solution," says Jesus, "is to look at your Father. He's awesome! He'll vindicate you and take care of you."

The fearless children of a fearsome Father

Jesus is not sending us a mixed message. He is not saying be afraid and don't be afraid, for there is no fear in love. Rather, he's putting persecution into perspective. He's saying:

Guys, it's natural to be scared of persecution and death. But there are scarier things out there. Your Father for One. He's the scariest *hombre* there is! And you have nothing to fear from him. When you understand this—when you know that God is *for* you and not against you—it will free you from the fear of men. So don't be afraid and don't worry. He who cares for the sparrows cares for you. And don't think you have to do any of this gospel stuff to earn your way into my kingdom. No, little flock, your Father is pleased to give you the kingdom.

Jesus came to free us from every fear. The disciples understood this which is why one of them later said:

> Do not fear their threats; do not be frightened. But in your hearts revere Christ as Lord. (1 Peter 3:14b–15a)

When you set apart Christ as Lord you are literally saying that Jesus is the ultimate power and authority. He is the *kurios*, the supreme ruler, and the final word on every subject. When fear comes to you, perhaps in the form of opposition or a bad doctor's report, this is the time to set apart Christ as Lord. This is the time to speak to your fears about the One who is above all and at whose name every knee will bow.

Be afraid of God? Not us, not his dearly beloved kids. But those enemies of his who hate Jesus and seek to intimidate and threaten his kids — yes, a little fear of the Lord might yet do them some good.

A word after

"Paul, I have been attending a revival meeting and the preacher has been talking about lukewarm, lackadaisical Christians being sent to hell. I felt luke-warm after hearing this and it left a bad taste in my mouth. But at the meeting I was prayed for and delivered from a serious health problem. Does this miracle prove that the message is true?"

No, it proves that God is gracious and that he doesn't wait for us to get our doctrinal ducks lined up before he blesses us.

It is the way of the world to stir up fear in order to sell you something. "You are lukewarm and in danger of hell! Repent, come forward, sign up, get busy." But it's not the way of heaven.

The kingdom of heaven is marked by right-eousness, peace and joy in the Holy Spirit (Romans 14:17). If the message you are listening to leads you to receive the free gift of Christ's righteousness, you can expect to have peace and joy. But if it doesn't, you won't.

The gospel of heaven testifies to the goodness of God and his gracious gifts. If the message you're hearing leaves you with a bad taste in your mouth, you can be sure it is not the gospel because God's gifts are flawless and good.

13. What is the Fear of the Lord?

I've had people tell me, "I walk in the love *and* the fear of God," by which they mean, "God is scary and will only accept me if I endure and overcome and obey and do all the other things the Bible says." Or they say, "God qualifies me, but I can disqualify myself through sin, doubt, or insufficient repentance. A holy fear of a bookkeeping God keeps me on the straight and narrow."

These statements sound pious but they're faithless. They belie a confidence in the flesh that is insulting to Jesus.

> There is no fear in love. But perfect love drives out fear, because fear has to do with punishment. The one who fears is not made perfect in love. (1 John 4:18)

Fear and love don't mix

If you fear the punishment or chastisement of God, then love has not had its perfect work in you. Look again to the cross. See the finished work. If God loved you and did all that for you while you were a sinner, what won't he do for you now? God is for you, not against you.

What is the fear of the Lord? Perhaps you've heard it said, "To fear God is to worship him." This interpretation comes from Jesus. Remember how he quoted scripture to silence the devil in the wilderness? Let's compare what Jesus said with the actual scripture he quoted:

What Jesus said: "It is written: 'Worship the Lord your God, and serve him only.'" (Matthew 4:10b)
The original text: "Fear the Lord your God and serve him only." (Deuteronomy 6:13a)

See the difference? Moses said, "Fear God," which Jesus interpreted as, "Worship him." So whenever you read an exhortation to fear the Lord in the Bible, you can interpret it as "worship the Lord." Jesus gives you permission.

"But Paul, 'through the fear of the Lord, men depart from evil.' It's only the fear of punishment that stops people from sinning."

That's good advice when dealing with two-year olds or stubborn Israelites. Under the old covenant, the fear of punishment was meant to keep people in line. If you didn't keep the rules, you got whacked.

But in the new covenant, you have already died (Colossians 3:3). Your old self is in the grave. Having been raised with Christ you are free to live fearlessly.

The Spirit of love

Fear has no place in a healthy, loving relationship. It's important that you get this for you cannot balance fear with love. You cannot have a part of your heart shouting, "I love you Lord" while another part whispers, "but I'm afraid of you." You will never give yourself wholly to someone you're afraid of.

If you ever hear a message that leaves you fearful and uncertain of your Father's love, reject it. It's anti-Christ poison. The words may be from the Bible, but the spirit behind it is not from the Lord. God has not given us a spirit of fear and intimidation, but a Spirit of love:

> And hope does not put us to shame, because
> God's love has been poured out into our hearts
> through the Holy Spirit (Romans 5:5a)

The Holy Spirit will always seek to remind you that you are God's dearly loved child.

"Sure, Paul, I get that. I know God loves everyone."

Not just everyone; he loves *you*. You need to make this personal. You need to see yourself as the apple of your Father's eye.

I encourage you to get into the habit of agreeing with the Holy Spirit. Tell yourself every day, "God loves me and there's nothing I can do to make him love me any more or any less." And as the love of God takes root and grows in your heart, it will drive out all fear. The phrase "Fear not" will become real to you. You won't fear failure, you won't fear men, you won't fear death, and you certainly won't fear your loving Father.

Unbelievers may fear, but the children of God are fearless. The wicked flee when none pursue but the righteous are as bold as a lion.

> But from everlasting to everlasting the Lord's love is with those who fear him. (Psalm 103:17a)

Only those who are secure in their Father's everlasting love know what it is to fear the Lord. It is to see him as he truly is and respond with awe-struck adoration. It is to tremble in his presence knowing he is surely good, he is surely supreme, and he surely loves me.

A word after

"Paul, you are forgetting the sternness and severity of God. Romans 11:22 says we're supposed to consider it, otherwise we might get cut off." I have no doubt that Romans 11 has been used to sow fear in the church, but that was never Paul's intention. Romans 11 isn't a warning to the church, but the Gentiles in general. "I am talking to you Gentiles" (Romans 11:13). He's saying the Gentiles have been given an opportunity to receive God's favor but like the Jews they may miss out on account of unbelief. He's not warning Christians; he's warning unbelievers.

Many scriptures have been used to terrorize the saints, but Paul's desire was that we might have an assurance of our Father's love and live free from fear.

The Spirit you received does not make you slaves, so that you live in fear again; rather, the Spirit you received brought about your adoption to sonship. And by him we cry, "Abba, Father." (Romans 8:15)

Before I understood grace, I tolerated a little fear of the Lord. I thought it was healthy. I thought it would keep me on the straight and narrow. But I have renewed my mind! There is no fear in love and we are not to be governed by fear. Not even a little bit. Jesus didn't suffer and die so that we might live in fear, but so that we might be free.

14. James—Preacher of Grace?

It seems everyone has an opinion about James and how his letter fits, or doesn't fit, into the New Testament. This week an E2R reader sent me a line from a commentator who basically said James was not on the same page as Paul when it came to the gospel of grace. Their letters do not line up because James did not get grace.

I can understand how a glance at one or two verses in James might give this impression. But do you really believe that 26 books in the New Testament preach the same gospel message while James preaches another?

Paul said if anyone preached a different gospel, that person should be accursed (Galatians 1:8–9). If James is preaching something different from Paul, then the New Testament writers are a house divided. And if *that* were the case, the Bible cannot be trusted.

I take a different view.

Grace and truth came through Jesus Christ. It is his gospel that the New Testament writers proclaimed. I'm going to present some scriptures side-by-side to show that not only were Paul and James on the same wavelength, but they both preached the good news exactly as Jesus modeled it.

Below is a list of statements that you might hear from any grace preacher. Under each statement I have pasted sound bites from Jesus, Paul, and James. As we will see, those things that mattered to Jesus, also mattered to Paul and James. They may say things a little differently, but they all say the same things.

1. Good news: God offers you his unmerited favor!

Jesus: "The Spirit of the Lord is on me, because he has anointed me to preach good news to the poor… to proclaim the year of the Lord's favor." (Luke 4:18a,19)

Paul: "For it is by grace you have been saved, through faith…" (Ephesians 2:8a)

James: "But he gives us more grace. That is why Scripture says: 'God opposes the proud but shows favor to the humble.'" (James 4:6)

2. Believe this good news …

Jesus: "Repent and believe the good news!" (Mark 1:15b)

Paul: "For I am not ashamed of the gospel, because it is the power of God that brings salvation to everyone who believes…" (Romans 1:16a)

James: "…humbly accept the word planted in you which can save you." (James 1:21b)

3. …and repent—change the way you think and live.

Jesus: "Therefore everyone who hears these words of mine and puts them into practice is like a wise man who built his house on the rock." (Matthew 7:24)

Paul: "I preached that they should repent and turn to God and demonstrate their repentance by their deeds." (Acts 26:20b)

James: "Do not merely listen to the word, and so deceive yourselves. Do what it says... Faith by itself, if it is not accompanied by action, is dead." (James 1:22, 2:17)

4. It is God who makes us acceptable...

Jesus: "For God did not send his Son into the world to condemn the world, but to save the world through him." (John 3:17)

Paul: "Giving joyful thanks to the Father, who has qualified you to share in the inheritance of his holy people..." (Colossians 1:12a)

James: "Humble yourselves before the Lord and he will lift you up." (James 4:10)

5. Now go and tell others the good news of God's grace!

Jesus: "Go into all the world and preach the gospel to all creation." (Mark 16:15)

Paul: "Do the work of an evangelist, discharge all the duties of your ministry." (2 Timothy 4:5b)

James: "Remember this: Whoever turns a sinner from the error of their way will save them from death and cover over a multitude of sins." (James 5:20)

As you can see, James was not marching to the beat of a different drummer. His message was essentially the same message that Jesus lived and Paul preached.

A word after

Several years ago, on a long drive home with Camilla, I was fired up with the thought that James has been dismissed as a grace ignoramus.

"James had a one-on-one encounter with the risen Lord (1 Corinthians 15:7). Paul was radically changed when he saw Jesus. Why do we think James wasn't?"

I was just getting warmed up.

"James was Paul's friend. Don't you think Paul would've said something if James was out of line? Paul confronted Peter, yet he never confronted James. He didn't need to. They were on the same page!"

I was so fired up it's amazing I didn't get a speeding ticket.

"Some people think they know Paul's gospel better than James did, but James heard it in the flesh (see Galatians 2:2). He got it straight from the source."

When I got home I sat down to write the first of what turned out to be a dozen articles on James. The article above was the last one in that series. (You can find the others in the E2R Archives.)

I am absolutely convinced that James understood the gospel of grace and the proof is in his letter. Read his epistle through the lens of the cross and you can't help but see Jesus.

15. The X-Men Gospel

In all literature, there may be only five or six great stories but these few stories are told again and again, a thousand different ways.

I was reminded of this while watching *X-Men: Days of Future Past*. (Warning: spoilers ahead!) On the surface, this is a film about saving the future by altering the past. But there is a deeper narrative here, and one that connects to a Greater Story that has been told again and again since the beginning of time. I am referring to the ancient struggle between a kingdom built on power, and another built on love. It's Satan vs Jesus, Anakin vs Obi-Wan, Gollum vs Frodo, and in the X-Men film, it's Erik vs Charles.

Erik, a.k.a. Magneto, is a powerful mutant who is determined to do whatever it takes to secure the future of his race. His friend, Charles, a.k.a. Professor Xavier, is a fellow mutant who dreams of a future characterized by peace between mutants and humans.

Erik/Magneto represents the kingdom of power. He's Herod, Caiaphas, and Caesar, all rolled into one.

Charles Xavier represents the kingdom of love. He's Martin Luther King, Gandhi, and Jesus, all rolled into one.

While Erik treads the path of power, Charles prefers the way of grace. Erik is a warrior; Charles is a healer. If Erik's goal is to make things right, Charles' goal is to make things beautiful.

The dramatic tension between Erik and Charles makes for a great story because it evokes two universal questions.

1. Do the ends justify the means?

In the X-Men movie, Erik is fighting for a cause and will do whatever it takes to accomplish his goal. Initially, we have some sympathy for his heavy-handed methods. After all, he's just trying to protect his mutant family. But when Erik himself starts killing mutants, we realize something has gone terribly wrong.

Erik's goal is not evil—he just wants his kind to live—but his methods are so brutal that other mutants describe him as a monster. In this and other X-Men films, Erik's strategies ultimately pit mutant against mutant, and brother against brother. This is a recurring theme in the kingdom of power. Cain kills Abel, Sméagol kills Déagol, Scar kills Mufasa, Michael Corleone kills Fredo, and Magneto's actions ultimately lead to the deaths of virtually every mutant, including himself.

What can we learn from this?

We repeat Magneto's mistake whenever we put a cause—a vision, a ministry, a career—ahead of people. Zeal for a goal can lead us to value people by how much they help us and shoot those who get in our way. We may tell ourselves that the outcome justifies the means—"I'm building the kingdom of God"—but we are really building the kingdom of Satan. Like Saul, who thought he was serving God, we are really persecuting Jesus (Acts 9:5).

Erik's methods are selfish and ugly and consequently any good he seeks to do becomes rotten. He's Anakin Skywalker sliding towards the dark side and he's Boromir of Gondor lusting for the ring of power. But ultimately he's Adam sewing fig leaves in a futile attempt to make things right.

Charles shows us a different path. For Charles, it is not enough that the dream is beautiful, the means must be beautiful as well. While Erik draws lines dividing us (those who are with me) from them (those who are against me), Charles reaches out and turns enemies into friends. He sees the good in others, even those who have lost their way, and he prophetically calls them towards their destiny.

2. Walk by faith or sight?

A seminal moment in the film occurs when Charles has a conversation with his older self. Young Charles is beginning to lose sight of his dream of peace. Humanity seems unredeemable and the future looks bleak. But Old Charles intervenes with words of grace and forgiveness: "Just because someone stumbles and loses their path, doesn't mean they can't be saved."

How does salvation come? How is a wrong put right? Not with power enforced by violence but with love. Justice isn't found down the barrel of a gun. It's made by peace-makers who embrace their enemies and resist those things which are opposed to love.

The success of the film is this: although Charles is more powerful than Erik, he does not win by engaging in a contest of strength. In the critical moment Charles lies crippled under a fallen steel beam, as helpless as a Savior on a cross. Yet even in the face of death, Charles refuses to wield his power. He doesn't call down his twelve legions of angels. Instead, he yields control, effectively laying down his life, by putting his faith in another.

Into the cataclysmic battle between power and love comes a broken and hurting woman. Raven represents fallen humanity. In an earlier film she ran from Charles to Erik only to be betrayed in this film. Now she has become Cain, a restless wanderer, with murder on her heart.

In the climactic scene Raven is about to assassinate a man who is a key player in the conflict between humanity and the mutants. Before she pulls the trigger, Charles calls to her:

> Raven, please don't do this!… I have faith in you, Raven. I believe you are not the kind of person humanity sees you to be. I've been trying to control you from the beginning… everything that happens now is in your hands.[6]

---

[6] Bryan Singer (director), *X-Men: Days of Future Past*. 2014. Twentieth Century Fox Film Corporation: USA.

Charles' faith in Raven turns the tide and breaks the cycle of violence and retribution. His act of love leads to a stunning reversal of all the harm done amounting to a resurrection, not only of those who died in this film, but also those who died in previous films. It is a jaw-dropping restoration.

What can we learn from the X-Men?

The X-Men movie shows us that power — whether defined as technology (represented by a mad military-scientist called Trask), politics (President Nixon), or superhuman abilities (Magneto) — becomes abusive when love is absent. Even when our goals are noble, an obsession with outcomes can blind us to the ugliness of our actions. And when we trust in our own strength and abilities, we limit our options and curse what we do (Jeremiah 17:5).

Charles, who represents a type of Jesus, shows us a better way. His faith in Raven reflects God's faith in us. God does not want to control you, he wants to love you. He wants the best for you and he is continually calling you towards your destiny.

Raven's choice is our choice. We can pull the trigger of power and try to make things happen in our own strength or we can respond to the call of grace. We can try and take the world by force, or we can inherit it with meekness and trust.

The greatest achievement of the *X-Men: Days of Future Past* is in showing the ultimate victory of the kingdom of love over the principalities and powers of this world. It's a good story because it's really a Great Story.

A word after

And we might say it is a *remixed* story. It's an old story retold with a new set of characters.

Of course, the X-Men movie is hardly unique in this regard. Most movies are remixes of old stories. Consider the Disney classics *Snow White, Pinocchio, Treasure Island,* and *Peter Pan*. None of them were original Disney creations. They were all old tales that received the Disney treatment.

We love remixed stories especially those that remind us of God's Great Story.

At the start of this book I mentioned the story of the Good Samaritan. At one level that's a good story about a good man doing a good deed. But at another level it's a great story because it's really about Jesus, whom we did not know, finding us and caring for us after we had been robbed and left for dead. Religion (represented by the Levite and the priest) did nothing to help, but Jesus bound up our wounds, paid all our expenses, because he is the true friend who loves us.

Do you see? Absent grace and the Good Samaritan is merely a good story. It might inspire you to be good to strangers, but that's about it. But read that story through the lens of grace and it becomes a great story of a great Savior. Now we are moved.

Now we are inspired. Now we are asking, "Who is this Jesus who loves me so? I want to know him more."

When told with grace, the stories, proverbs, poems, and even the commands of the Bible, lead us to new revelation. They lift us to heaven and lead us to Jesus.

If you enjoyed this book, why not subscribe to E2R and get more articles just like these sent to your email. It's free! Sign up at:

escapetoreality.org/subscribe

Collect the Whole Set!

Grace Disco: E2R – Greatest Hits, Vol. 1
Is God's love unconditional? / God is good, but how good is he? / Son, servant or friend of God? / How well did I understand grace before I understood grace? / The top twelve blessings in the new covenant / The cure for guilt / What is holiness? / Does God use correction fluid? / Faith is a rest / Take up your cross daily / *and more!*

Grace Classics: E2R – Greatest Hits, Vol. 2
By which gospel are you saved? / Are you religious? / Does God give and take away? / Seven signs you might be under law / When doing good is bad for you / How to walk after the flesh in twenty easy lessons / Where was God in the Connecticut school shooting? / What happens to Christians who commit suicide? / *and more!*

Grace Party: E2R – Greatest Hits, Vol. 3
The gospel in one word, two words… / God believes in you! / Are you hot enough for God? / Ten myths about the Holy Spirit / Healthy vs unhealthy confession / What is the unforgivable sin? / What was Last Adam's greater work? / Can unbelievers take communion / Building ramps for the mentally ill / *and more!*

AVAILABLE NOW!

Amazon, BAM!, Barnes & Noble, Book Depository, Booktopia, Eden.co.uk, Kinokuniya, Loot.co.za, Nile.com.au, Waterstones, W.H. Smith, and other good retailers!

98877715R00061

Made in the USA
Lexington, KY
10 September 2018